WeightWatchers®
Deeply
Delicious

SIMON &
SCHUSTER

LONDON · NEW YORK · SYDNEY · TORONTO

First published in Great Britain by Simon & Schuster UK Ltd, 2008
A CBS Company

Copyright © 2008 Weight Watchers International, Inc.
All right reserved.
First published 2008
Simon and Schuster Illustrated
Simon & Schuster UK Ltd
222 Gray's Inn Road
London WC1X 8HB

10 9 8 7 6 5 4

Weight Watchers and **POINTS** are the registered trademarks
of Weight Watchers International Inc. and are used under
its control by Weight Watchers (UK) Ltd.

Weight Watchers Publications Team: Jane Griffiths,
Donna Watts, Nina McKerlie and Nina Bhogal

Photography by Steve Baxter, Iain Bagwell and Steve Lee
Design and typesetting by Fiona Andreanelli
Printed and bound in Singapore

A CIP catalogue for this book is available from the British
Library

ISBN 9 781847 371522

Pictured on the front cover: Raspberry tart, page 96.
Pictured on the back cover: Sweet pumpkin and peanut
curry page 89 (top left), Chocolate mocha mousse page 139
(top right), Sweetcorn and crab soup page 25 (bottom left),
French ham and bean casserole page 40 (bottom right)

 You'll find this easy to read **POINTS®** value logo
on every recipe throughout the book. The logo
represents the number of **POINTS** values per
serving each recipe contains.
The easy to use **POINTS** **Plan** is designed to help you
eat what you want – as long as you stay within your daily
POINTS allowance – giving you the freedom to enjoy the
food you love.

V This symbol denotes a vegetarian recipe and assumes
that, where relevant, organic eggs, vegetarian cheese and
vegetarian low fat crème fraîche is used. Virtually fat free
fromage frais may contain traces of gelatine so they are
not always vegetarian. Please check the labels.

❄ This symbol denotes a dish that can be frozen.

RECIPE NOTES:
All fruits, vegetables and eggs are medium sized unless
otherwise stated.

Raw eggs: Only the freshest eggs should be used.
Pregnant women, the elderly and children should avoid
recipes with eggs that are not fully cooked or raw.

Recipe timings are approximate and meant to be
guidelines. Please note that the preparation time includes
all the steps up to and following the main cooking time (s).

Contents

Deeply Delicious is the latest collection of recipes from Weight Watchers, full of healthy options, fresh ingredients and inspiration. With *Deeply Delicious* you'll find plenty of ideas to choose from, whether you're treating yourself to a leisurely weekend breakfast, comforting winter warmer, sweet treat, light lunch or quick and easy supper. There are also mouth-watering vegetarian recipes and variations.

Deeply Delicious is the ideal cookbook if you are looking to eat healthily. And with a range of recipes that are certain to suit the whole family, you can enjoy mealtimes without compromising your weight loss. With so many fabulous recipes to try, many are certain to become firm favourites.

Hot peppered chicken salad, page 42

Fluffy breakfast pancakes

Makes **10** small pancakes **V**

| **POINTS** values per recipe | 9½ | calories per serving | 155 |

These are like the pancakes that you get in America for breakfast in huge portions with maple syrup and bacon or sausages. This is a scrumptious low POINTS value version. Preparation and cooking time 25 minutes

2 medium eggs, separated
100 g (3½ oz) plain flour
½ teaspoon salt
2 teaspoons baking powder
2 teaspoons caster sugar
150 ml (5 fl oz) skimmed milk
low fat cooking spray

1 Gently heat a large frying pan or griddle. Whisk the egg whites until stiff. In a large bowl, sift the flour, salt, baking powder and sugar and mix together.

2 In a jug, beat the egg yolks and milk together. Pour this mixture into the dry ingredients and stir until just mixed but do not beat.

3 With a metal spoon, lightly fold in the egg whites. Spray the pan with the low fat cooking spray and drop the batter on to it in tablespoonfuls. You should be able to cook 3–4 at the same time.

4 After 1–2 minutes they should be puffed up and bubbly. Flip them over with a palette knife or fish slice and lightly brown the other side.

5 Keep them warm in a low heated oven on a plate covered with foil or a tea towel until they are all cooked.

Tropical fruit kebabs

Serves **4 V**

| **POINTS** values per recipe | 11 | calories per serving | 143 |

Preparation time 20 minutes

4 figs, halved
½ pineapple, cut into segments
8 large strawberries
2 bananas, cut into 2.5 cm (1 inch) lengths
2 peaches, quartered
juice and grated zest of 2 oranges
200 g (7 oz) low fat yogurt in any flavour, to serve

1 Soak 8 wooden kebab sticks in water for at least 10 minutes to prevent them from burning.

2 Thread 5 or 6 pieces of fruit on to each of the 8 wooden kebab sticks and place the kebabs in a large, shallow dish.

3 Mix the juice and grated zest together and pour over the kebabs. Leave to marinate for 10 minutes before placing under a grill or on a barbecue. Cook until the fruit starts to soften and turn golden at the edges. Serve with a bowl of low fat yogurt for dipping.

Start the day

Crispy potato cakes

Serves **4** ❄

| **POINTS** values per recipe | 8½ | calories per serving | 165 |

This makes an excellent brunch when you want something a little bit different. If you like, dish up each serving (2 cakes) with a poached egg on top. This will add 1½ **POINTS** values per serving.
Preparation and cooking time 25 minutes + 10 minutes cooling

225 g (8 oz) carrots
450 g (1 lb) floury potatoes, peeled but left whole
1 egg, beaten
1 tablespoon chopped fresh parsley
low fat cooking spray
150 g (5½ oz) turkey rashers
salt and freshly ground black pepper

1 Simmer the carrots and potatoes in lightly salted, boiling water for 5 minutes. Drain and let them cool for about 10 minutes, and then grate them coarsely.

2 Mix the grated carrot and potato with the egg, parsley and seasoning.

3 Heat a heavy frying pan until very hot and spray it with a little low fat cooking spray. Place 8 large tablespoons of the mixture in the pan, leaving a little space between each one. Flatten them a little with the back of a spoon. You may need to do all this in 2 batches.

4 Cook over a low heat for 5 minutes on each side, until the potato cakes are golden and cooked through.

5 Meanwhile, grill the turkey rashers until crispy. Serve 2 cakes per person topped with the crispy rashers.

TOP TIP It's quite important to use a floury potato such as Desirée for this recipe – waxy ones will not give the same results.

All in one breakfast omelette

Serves **1**

| **POINTS** values per recipe | **5** | calories per serving | **315** |

This is a delicious and healthy breakfast; it's a great kickstart to the day! *Preparation and cooking time 30 minutes*

25 g (1 oz) lean back bacon rasher
1 teaspoon sunflower oil
100 g (3½ oz) mushrooms, sliced
1 tomato, sliced
2 eggs
2 tablespoons skimmed milk
salt and freshly ground black pepper

1 Preheat the grill to a medium heat. Grill the bacon until it is crispy. Cut it into strips.
2 Heat the sunflower oil in a small non stick frying pan and add the mushrooms. Cook for 5 minutes, until they are softened and then add the tomato slices. Cook for a further 2 minutes. Remove them from the pan and set aside.
3 Whisk the eggs with the milk and seasoning and pour this into the pan. Cook for 2–3 minutes until you see the edges of the egg setting. Using a wooden spatula, draw the cooked egg into the centre of the pan, allowing the runny, uncooked egg to run to the edges.
4 When the egg is nearly set, arrange the cooked mushrooms, tomato and strips of grilled bacon on one side of the omelette. Using a spatula, flip the clear half of the omelette over the filling. Carefully slide it on to a warmed serving plate and eat at once.

VEGETARIAN OPTION Make sure you use free-range eggs and use a soya bacon rasher instead. Soya bacon rashers are readily available in supermarkets, but remember to alter the **POINTS** values accordingly.

Breakfast salad

Serves **4**

| **POINTS** values per recipe | **16½** | calories per serving | **185** |

This substantial salad is perfect for a lunchtime treat or brunch to stave off those hunger pangs. *Preparation time 15 minutes l Cooking time 15 minutes*

225 g (8 oz) low fat sausages
150 g (5½ oz) lean back bacon
low fat cooking spray
225 g (8 oz) open cup mushrooms, sliced
225 g (8 oz) cherry tomatoes, halved
1 tablespoon wholegrain mustard
1 tablespoon dark soy sauce
1 teaspoon clear honey
350 g (12 oz) iceberg lettuce, shredded

1 Grill the sausages for about 10 minutes until evenly browned and cooked through, and grill the bacon until crispy. Slice the sausages into rings and chop the bacon into small pieces.
2 Meanwhile, spray a frying pan with the low fat cooking spray and add the mushrooms. Cook them for 5 minutes until they are tender. Add the tomatoes, mustard, soy sauce and honey, and cook for a further 2 minutes, stirring occasionally. Add the sausages and bacon, and mix everything well.
3 Divide the Iceberg lettuce between 4 serving plates and top with the 'breakfast' mix. Serve at once.

VEGETARIAN OPTION Omit the bacon and use vegetarian sausages instead. The **POINTS** value will be 2 per serving.

The big brunch

Serves **1**

| **POINTS** values per recipe | 5½ | calories per serving | 385 |

Why not spoil yourself over a leisurely weekend brunch? It will set you up for the day! And it's a really relaxed way of entertaining. *Preparation and cooking time 15 minutes*

1 teaspoon vegetable oil
150 g (5½ oz) canned cooked potatoes or leftover boiled potatoes, sliced thickly
½ small onion, sliced thinly
75 g (2¾ oz) cooked beetroot, chopped into small pieces
50 g (1¾ oz) thick slice of cooked ham, cut into strips
1 egg, poached
1 tablespoon half fat crème fraîche
½ teaspoon horseradish relish

1 Heat the oil in a small frying pan. Fry the potatoes and onion over a high heat until browned. Stir in the beetroot and ham and gently heat through for 5 minutes.
2 Poach the egg until lightly set. Mix together the crème fraîche and horseradish.
3 Spoon the potato mixture on to a hot plate. Top with the poached egg and drizzle on the dressing. Serve.

TOP TIP This makes a tasty supper dish too.

VARIATIONS Replace the ham with sliced chicken or turkey breast. Smoked haddock fillet (100 g/3½ oz) is delicious, too. The **POINTS** values per serving will be 5½ with chicken, 6 with turkey and 5 with haddock.

Chilli corn fritters

Serves **4**

| **POINTS** values per recipe | 13 | calories per serving | 170 |

You can prepare these tasty cakes up to 2 days before you want to eat them, then just heat through to serve. *Preparation and cooking time 15 minutes*

50 g (1¾ oz) polenta
200 g (7 oz) canned sweetcorn
1 teaspoon chilli flakes
3 tablespoons chopped fresh coriander
1 tablespoon Thai green curry paste
1 tablespoon fish sauce
1 egg
1 tablespoon sunflower oil

1 Place the polenta in a mixing bowl and stir in the canned sweetcorn, chilli flakes, coriander, curry paste, fish sauce and egg. Mix together thoroughly until you have a combined sloppy mixture.
2 Heat a little oil in a frying pan, then drop spoonfuls of the mixture into the pan. Cook over a medium low heat for 3 to 4 minutes per side, until cooked through and golden.

VARIATION You can serve these cakes with a cucumber salad to complement their spiciness. Peel and halve a cucumber lengthways. Scoop out the seeds, dice the flesh and mix with 1 tablespoon of rice wine vinegar and a pinch of caster sugar.

Smoked haddock kedgeree

Serves **4**

| **POINTS** values per recipe | 19½ | calories per serving | 393 |

A classic recipe using smoked haddock, this kedgeree is tasty and substantial. If you keep some smoked haddock fillets in the freezer, try the kedgeree for an impromptu Sunday brunch or quick supper standby. *Preparation time 20 minutes l Cooking time 30–35 minutes*

300 g (10½ oz) smoked haddock fillets

2 bay leaves

4 whole peppercorns

300 ml (½ pint) skimmed milk

low fat cooking spray

2 onions, chopped

225 g (8 oz) basmati rice

a pinch of saffron threads, soaked in 2 tablespoons boiling
water for 2 minutes

1 tablespoon garam masala

700 ml (1¼ pints) chicken or vegetable stock

a large bunch of fresh parsley, chopped finely, stalks included

200 g (7 oz) very low fat plain fromage frais

salt and freshly ground black pepper

2 eggs, hard boiled and quartered, to garnish

1 lemon, cut into wedges, to garnish

1 Place the haddock fillets skin side up in a large pan with the bay leaves and peppercorns. Pour over the milk and bring to the boil; then turn off and leave to cool.

2 Meanwhile, heat a large non stick frying pan or wok and spray with the low fat cooking spray. Fry the onions until golden and softened, adding a little water if necessary to prevent them from sticking.

3 Add the rice, saffron threads with their soaking water and the garam masala, stirring to mix. Then add the stock and bring to the boil, stirring occasionally. Turn down to a gentle simmer and leave to cook for 15 minutes.

4 Remove the haddock from the milk and flake with your fingers on to a plate, removing the skin and any bones you find as you go. Strain the milk, add it to the rice and stir in.

5 After about 15–20 minutes, when the rice is just cooked and most of the liquid absorbed, add the flaked haddock, parsley and fromage frais. Stir to heat through. Check the seasoning and serve garnished with the egg and lemon wedges.

Bacon and mushroom risotto

Serves **2**

| **POINTS** values per recipe | 16½ | calories per serving | 450 |

An easy brunch or supper dish made from rice cooked in stock with mushrooms and crispy bacon. *Preparation time 20 minutes l Cooking time 25 minutes*

4 medium rashers of lean back bacon

100 g (3½ oz) mushrooms, sliced

juice of 1 lemon

2 dried mushrooms (porcini), soaked in 150 ml (5 fl oz) boiling
    water for 10 minutes

low fat cooking spray

1 medium onion, chopped finely

175 g (6 oz) risotto rice

150 ml (5 fl oz) white wine

300 ml (½ pint) hot stock

a small bunch of parsley, chopped

salt and freshly ground black pepper

1 Preheat the grill to high, grill the bacon until crispy then chop into little pieces. Set to one side. Meanwhile, heat a frying pan and add the sliced mushrooms. Season and stir fry for 5 minutes then add the lemon juice and cook for 1 minute until absorbed. Set aside.

2 Drain the porcini, reserving the soaking liquid. Chop finely and add to the cooked mushrooms.

3 Heat a saucepan and spray with the low fat cooking spray then fry the onion for 4 minutes, until softened. Add the rice, stir, then pour in the wine and porcini soaking liquid and stir vigorously. Add the warmed stock a ladleful at a time after the stock is absorbed, which should take about 5 minutes. Stir between each addition. It will take around 20 minutes before all the stock is absorbed.

4 Stir in the cooked mushrooms, bacon and chopped parsley, check the seasoning and then serve.

VARIATION Serve with a few shavings of fresh Parmesan (10 g/¼ oz) per person) and add 1 **POINTS** value per serving.

Mango and raspberry smoothie

Serves **2 V**

| **POINTS** values per recipe | 4 | calories per serving | 148 |

If you're struggling to find ways to eat all of your 5 a day fruit and vegetable portions, a homemade smoothie is an easy way to boost your intake, and it tastes fabulous too. *Preparation and cooking time 5 minutes*

4 large ice cubes
150 ml (5 fl oz) skimmed milk
1 ripe medium mango, peeled, stoned and chopped roughly
1 ripe medium banana, chopped roughly
100 g (3½ oz) frozen raspberries
juice of ½ lemon

1 Place the first five ingredients listed in a liquidiser and blend until smooth, and then add lemon juice to taste.
2 Divide between two tall glasses, add drinking straws and serve immediately.

5 A DAY Using whole fruits in a smoothie means that you get all the healthy fibre, so it's better for you than fruit juice.

TOP TIP To prepare a mango, start by removing the skin with a vegetable peeler. Mangoes have a large flat stone in the middle, so slice down each side of the stone with a knife to remove most of the flesh, then cut away any mango still attached around the stone.

Oven-roasted tomato tartlets

Makes **8 V** ❋ *Roasted tomatoes only*

| **POINTS** values per recipe | 10 | calories per serving | 120 |

Slow roasting tomatoes brings out their wonderful rich flavour. *Preparation time 15 minutes l Cooking time 1¼ hours*

1 kg (2 lb 4 oz) plum tomatoes
1 teaspoon salt
8 sheets of filo pastry
2 tablespoons olive oil
2 tablespoons fresh basil leaves, torn (optional)
freshly ground black pepper

1 Preheat the oven to Gas Mark 2/150°C/fan oven 130°C.
2 Slice the tomatoes in half horizontally and arrange cut-side up on a cooling rack. Lift the cooling rack over a baking sheet and then sprinkle the salt over the tomatoes.
3 Roast the tomatoes in the oven for 1 hour, until they are beginning to dry out a little.
4 After the tomatoes have cooked, increase the oven temperature to Gas Mark 5/190°C/fan oven 170°C. Cut each sheet of filo pastry in half, brush with olive oil and sandwich two halves together. Press into 8 individual tartlet tins scrunching up the edges with your fingers so the pastry fits into the tins. Brush the insides of the tartlet cases with any remaining olive oil and place a crumpled piece of foil into each one. Bake for 15 minutes, until the pastry is crisp and golden.
5 Carefully remove the pastry cases from the tins, remove the foil and fill with the roasted tomato halves.
6 Scatter each tartlet with a little torn basil, if using, and a generous grinding of black pepper.

TOP TIP It's better to tear fresh basil rather than chop it, since this prevents it from bruising.

Rancher's turkey

Serves **2**

| **POINTS** values per recipe | 14½ | calories per serving | 455 |

A tasty, filling supper for all those hungry ranchers out there. *Preparation and cooking time 15 minutes*

2 turkey breast fillets, weighing 175 g (6 oz) each
low fat cooking spray
1 large tomato, chopped finely
2 tablespoons hickory BBQ sauce
2 medium lean, rindless, smoked streaky bacon rashers
400 g can baked beans
1 tablespoon Worcestershire sauce
salt and freshly ground black pepper

1 Place the turkey fillets between two sheets of clingfilm then beat with a rolling pin until flattened to an even thickness and season on both sides. Heat a large frying pan and spray with the low fat cooking spray, add the turkey fillets and fry for 2 minutes on each side.

2 Preheat the grill. Mix the tomato with the BBQ sauce. Place the turkey fillets on the grill pan lined with foil, and top each with the tomato mixture and then a piece of bacon.

3 Grill for 3 minutes until the bacon is crispy. Meanwhile, heat the baked beans and stir in the Worcestershire sauce. Pile on to serving plates and top with the turkey.

Gammon and egg with parsley sauce

Serves **4**

| **POINTS** values per recipe | 34 | calories per serving | 332 |

This dish goes well with crunchy green vegetables and potatoes mashed with skimmed milk. *Preparation and cooking time 20 minutes*

150 g (5½ oz) low fat fromage frais
75 g (2¾ oz) low fat soft cheese
3 tablespoons chopped fresh parsley
4 gammon steaks
4 eggs
salt and freshly ground black pepper

1 Whisk together the fromage frais and soft cheese. Heat gently in a small pan and stir in the parsley and seasoning.

2 Heat a grill to medium-high and cook the gammon steaks for 6–7 minutes on each side.

3 Poach the eggs.

4 Serve each gammon steak with a poached egg on top, with the parsley sauce spooned over.

Raspberry yogurt muffins

Makes **12 V** ❄

| **POINTS** values per recipe | 33½ | calories per serving | 190 |

Muffins are a treat that come from the USA, although you might find that they are twice the size on the other side of the Atlantic! We've made these smaller versions to help keep the **POINTS** values under control. *Preparation time 15 minutes l Cooking time 15–20 minutes*

300 g (10½ oz) plain white flour
2 teaspoons baking powder
½ teaspoon ground cinnamon
150 g (5½ oz) light muscovado sugar
100 g (3½ oz) fresh raspberries
1 egg
150 g (5½ oz) low fat plain yogurt
150 ml (5 fl oz) skimmed milk
3 tablespoons sunflower oil

1 Preheat the oven to Gas Mark 6/200°C/fan oven 180°C. Line a 12 hole muffin tray with paper muffin cases, or use squares of greaseproof paper pushed into the holes.
2 Sift the flour, baking powder and cinnamon into a large mixing bowl. Stir in the sugar and raspberries.
3 Beat the egg, yogurt, milk and oil together, and then stir this into the dry ingredients, taking care not to over mix. Spoon the muffin mixture into the paper cases.
4 Bake for 15–20 minutes, until the muffins are risen and golden brown. Cool in the tray for a few minutes, and then transfer the muffins to a wire rack to cool completely.

TOP TIP The secret of successful muffins is to avoid beating the mixture too much when you add the wet ingredients to the dry ones. They need to be lightly stirred together until just combined.

VARIATION Use 100 g (3½ oz) fresh blueberries instead of raspberries. The **POINTS** values per serving will remain the same.

Spicy banana muffins

Makes **10 V** ❄ *up to 1 month*

| **POINTS** values per recipe | 24 | calories per serving | 165 |

A great way to start the day. *Preparation time 15 minutes l Cooking time 20–25 minutes*

50 g (1¾ oz) low fat spread
200 g (7 oz) plain flour
2 teaspoons baking powder
100 g (3½ oz) caster sugar
1 teaspoon ground cinnamon
2 bananas
juice of 1 lemon
100 ml (3½ fl oz) skimmed milk
1 egg, beaten

1 Preheat the oven to Gas Mark 6/200°C/fan oven 180°C. Put 10 paper muffin cases into a muffin tin.

2 Melt the low fat spread and leave to cool slightly.

3 Sift the dry ingredients into a large bowl.

4 Mash the bananas with a fork and 1 teaspoon of the lemon juice.

5 Mix together the remaining lemon juice, milk and egg.

6 Pour the wet ingredients into the dry ones and stir very carefully – do not over mix.

7 Gently fold in the mashed banana and then divide the mixture between the paper muffin cases.

8 Cook in the preheated oven for 20–25 minutes until golden. Cool on a rack or eat slightly warm – delicious!

Curried parsnip soup

Serves **4 V** ❄ *recommended for up to 1 month*

| **POINTS** values per recipe | 4 | calories per serving | 65 |

Nothing beats a home made, warming soup, perfect to perk you up on a cold winter's day.
Preparation time 15 minutes l Cooking time 18–20 minutes

low fat cooking spray
1 onion, chopped
400 g (14 oz) parsnips, peeled and chopped
1 teaspoon curry powder
1 teaspoon ground ginger
1 teaspoon ground cumin
850 ml (1½ pints) vegetable stock
salt and freshly ground black pepper

1 Spray a medium saucepan with low fat cooking spray and sauté the onion for 4–5 minutes until beginning to soften.
2 Add the parsnips and spices and stir well to coat the vegetables with the spices.
3 Pour in the stock, season, bring to the boil and then simmer for 18–20 minutes, until the parsnips are tender.
4 Take off the heat and leave to cool for a couple of minutes.
5 When slightly cooled, blend the soup with a hand blender or in a food processor.
6 Check the seasoning, reheat and serve.

VARIATION For a zero **POINTS** value alternative, try curried cauliflower soup. Just substitute a medium cauliflower for the parsnips and follow the method above.

Chunky tomato soup

Serves **4 V** *without the Worcestershire sauce* ❄ *see tip*

| **POINTS** values per recipe | 2½ | calories per serving | 85 |

The delicate, peppery taste of the rocket leaves make this tomato soup taste fabulous.
Preparation time 15 minutes l Cooking time 25 minutes

low fat cooking spray
1 onion, chopped finely
2 garlic cloves, crushed
400 g can of chopped tomatoes
300 ml (10 fl oz) tomato juice
300 ml (10 fl oz) vegetable stock
1 tablespoon Worcestershire sauce
salt and freshly ground black pepper
100 ml (3½ fl oz) low fat plain fromage frais
100 g (3½ oz) rocket leaves, to serve

1 Spray a large saucepan with low fat cooking spray, and add the onion and garlic. Cook over a low heat, stirring from time to time, until the onion has softened but not browned, adding a little water if it sticks. This will take about 10 minutes.
2 Add the chopped tomatoes, tomato juice, stock and Worcestershire sauce, and bring to the boil. Reduce the heat, cover and simmer for 15 minutes. Season to taste.
3 Stir in the fromage frais and then ladle the soup into four warmed bowls. Alternatively, you can top the soup with a spoonful of fromage frais (about ½ a tablespoon per serving). Scatter over the rocket leaves, and serve.

TOP TIP This soup freezes well, but do freeze it before you add the fromage frais. When you are ready to serve, reheat the soup and then continue from step 3.

Light lunches

Greek potato patties (potato kephtedes)

Serves **4 V**

| **POINTS** values per recipe | **12** | calories per serving | **235** |

These spicy Greek patties are delicious served with a yogurt and cucumber dip. *Preparation time 30 minutes + chilling l Cooking time 40 minutes*

750 g (1 lb 10 oz) potatoes, peeled and chopped

low fat cooking spray

a bunch of spring onions, sliced finely

1 red chilli, de-seeded and chopped finely

1 tablespoon olive oil

1 egg, beaten

a small bunch of mint, chopped roughly

salt and freshly ground black pepper

1 Bring a large pan of water to the boil and then cook the potatoes for 20 minutes or until tender. Drain, then mash and season.

2 Spray a large frying pan with the cooking spray, then sauté the onions and chilli for 2 minutes. Add a tablespoon of water if they stick.

3 Mix the onions and chilli together with the olive oil, egg and mint into the potato. Season and leave to cool for 20 minutes.

4 Preheat the grill to medium and shape the potato mixture into 8 patties. Place on a foil-lined grill pan.

5 Grill the patties for 5 minutes on each side or until golden.

Stuffed cabbage leaves (dolmades)

Serves **4 V** ❄

| **POINTS** values per recipe | **13½** | calories per serving | **260** |

Authentic Greek 'dolmades' are wrapped in vine or fig leaves but this recipe has been adapted to use the more readily available Savoy cabbage leaves. Cabbage leaves also allow for more filling! Serve hot or cold with lemon slices and fresh dill sprigs or mint, or with Tzatziki.

Preparation time 1 hour l Cooking time 1 hour

2 tablespoons pine kernels

16 leaves of Savoy cabbage

125 g (4½ oz) long grain rice, uncooked

1 onion, chopped finely

8 dried apricots, chopped finely

4 tablespoons chopped fresh parsley

4 tablespoons chopped fresh dill

4 tablespoons chopped fresh mint

zest and juice of 1 lemon

1 tablespoon olive oil

sea salt and freshly ground black pepper

1 Put the pine kernels in a dry frying pan and toast over a low heat until they are beginning to brown. Keep an eye on them to make sure that they don't burn.

2 Wash the the cabbage leaves, then blanch them in batches of 5 or 6 in boiling, salted water for 5 seconds. Take them out with tongs and drain.

3 Mix all the remaining ingredients together in a bowl.

4 Line the base of a large saucepan with a couple of cabbage leaves. To fill the other leaves, place 1 or 2 tablespoons of the stuffing at the stalk end of the leaf and roll once. Then fold in the sides and continue to roll. Secure with cocktail sticks and put in the saucepan. When one layer is complete, sprinkle over some seasoning and then start another.

5 When all the leaves are used up, place a small inverted plate inside the saucepan and over the top of the stuffed leaves to weigh them all down. Carefully add 425 ml (¾ pint) boiling water to the pan. Cover and simmer for 50 minutes.

Salmon and avocado jackets

Serves **4**

| **POINTS** values per recipe | **19** | calories per serving | **290** |

For a quick and tasty filling for jacket potatoes, Mrs Hallin, a Gold Member from Southsea in Hampshire, whizzes together a few ingredients in her blender and the result is a very tasty light lunch or supper dish. *Preparation time 5 minutes l Cooking time 1 hour*

4 medium baking potatoes
100 g (3½ oz) smoked salmon trimmings
½ medium avocado
200 g can of tuna in brine or water, drained
2 teaspoons balsamic vinegar
25 g (1 oz) Quark
freshly ground black pepper
chopped fresh parsley or coriander, to garnish

1 Preheat the oven to Gas Mark 6/200°C/fan oven 180°C.
2 Bake the potatoes for approximately 1 hour, until tender.
3 A few minutes before the potatoes are ready, put the salmon trimmings, avocado, tuna, vinegar and Quark into a food processor or blender and whizz together for a few seconds until smooth. Season to taste with a little black pepper.
4 Make a deep cut in the top of the potatoes, push open and fill with an equal amount of the filling. Serve at once, garnished with chopped fresh parsley or coriander.

TOP TIP For a chunkier texture, simply mix together all the filling ingredients with a fork.

VARIATIONS You can use lemon or lime juice instead of balsamic vinegar, if you prefer. Instead of using the avocado mixture to fill jacket potatoes, serve with 2 medium slices of hot toast per person. The **POINTS** values per serving will be 4.

Sweetcorn and crab Soup

Serves **4**

| **POINTS** values per recipe | **7½** | calories per serving | **135** |

A delicious soup filled with sweetcorn and crab – great as a starter or even a light lunch. *Preparation time 5 minutes l Cooking time 10 minutes*

1 egg white
1 teaspoon sesame oil
1.2 litres (2 pints) chicken stock
275 g (9½ oz) canned or frozen sweetcorn
1 tablespoon soy sauce
2 teaspoons chopped fresh root ginger
2 teaspoons cornflour, mixed with 2 teaspoons water
225 g (8 oz) canned crabmeat
4 spring onions, chopped
freshly ground black pepper

1 Beat the egg white and sesame oil together and leave to one side.
2 Bring the stock to the boil in a large pan and add the sweetcorn. Simmer for 5 minutes and then add the soy sauce, ginger, pepper and cornflour paste.
3 Bring back to the boil, lower the heat to a simmer and add the crabmeat.
4 Slowly pour in the egg white and sesame oil mixture, stirring constantly.
5 Sprinkle over the spring onions and serve.

TOP TIP When buying fresh ginger, always select firm, unshrivelled pieces and peel off the skin before use.

VARIATION Chicken and sweetcorn soup can be made in the same way – substitute the same amount of cooked shredded chicken for the crab meat. The **POINTS** values per serving will be 2½.

Quick mushroom pizza stack

Serves **1 V**

| **POINTS** values per recipe | **3½** | calories per serving | **290** |

Big juicy field mushrooms are ideal for this quick pizza and taste delicious smothered in cheese.
Preparation and cooking time 10 minutes

low fat cooking spray
2 large flat mushrooms
½ onion, sliced thinly
1 slice wholemeal bread
1 tablespoon low fat cream cheese
25 g (1 oz) grated mozzarella light
½ teaspoon chives, snipped, to garnish

1 Spray a frying pan with low fat cooking spray and when it is hot, add the mushrooms and onion and cook for 5 minutes until browned. Set aside.
2 Preheat the grill to medium and toast one side of the bread until golden. Spread the cream cheese over the untoasted side of the bread.
3 Top with the mushrooms, onions and mozzarella and grill for 1–2 minutes until the cheese is bubbling and the toast browned. Garnish with the snipped chives.

TOP TIP Field mushrooms or large flat mushrooms are big and juicy. If you can't get hold of them, use 75 g (2¾ oz) of the closed cup variety.

Chilli seafood spaghetti

Serves **4**

| **POINTS** values per recipe | **16½** | calories per serving | **305** |

A great pasta dish with a lovely spicy tomato and seafood sauce. *Preparation time 6 minutes l Cooking time 10 minutes*

200 g (7 oz) spaghetti
low fat cooking spray
1 onion, chopped
¼ teaspoon chilli flakes
400 g (14 oz) canned chopped tomatoes
300 g (10½ oz) mixed seafood
2 tablespoons chopped fresh parsley
salt and freshly ground black pepper
50 g (1¾ oz) half fat Cheddar cheese, grated, to serve

1 Bring a pan of salted water to the boil and then add the spaghetti and cook for 6–8 minutes until al dente (tender but still with a slight 'bite').
2 Meanwhile in another pan, heat the low fat cooking spray and sauté the onion for 3–4 minutes and then add the chilli flakes.
3 Pour in the chopped tomatoes and cook for 1–2 minutes. Then add the mixed seafood. Stir in the chopped parsley.
4 When the pasta is cooked, drain and add to the seafood mixture. Toss gently to coat the pasta with the sauce, check the seasoning, and then divide between four pasta bowls. Sprinkle with the grated cheese and serve immediately.

TOP TIP If you like your food slightly hotter, just add more chilli flakes.

VARIATION This can be made into a more substantial meal by adding 50 g (1¾ oz) of prawns or chopped salami. The **POINTS** values per serving will be 4½ if using prawns or 5½ if using salami.

French sandwich (pan bagnat)

Serves **6**

| **POINTS** values per recipe | **14** | calories per serving | **205** |

This was created in France for labourers to take out to the fields for lunch. *Preparation time 10 minutes + 2 hours infusing time*

6 medium crusty rolls
2 tablespoons white wine vinegar or lemon juice
2 garlic cloves, crushed
4 tomatoes, sliced thinly
1 onion
2 red pepper, de-seeded and cut into thin strips
2 x 200 g cans of tuna in brine
a large handful of basil, torn coarsely
black olives (optional)
sea salt and freshly ground pepper

1 Slice the rolls in half horizontally. Drizzle the vinegar or lemon juice over the cut faces of the bread. Scatter the garlic and seasoning on top.
2 Arrange the vegetables, tuna, basil and olives, if using, on one half of each roll and then place the other half on top. Wrap the rolls in foil or a clean tea towel. Place a weight, such as a breadboard, on top and leave for at least 2 hours before serving.

VEGETARIAN OPTIONS You could replace the tuna with 200 g (7 oz) vegetarian low fat cheese. The **POINTS** values per serving would be 3½. You could also add 12 black olives in step 2. The **POINTS** values will remain the same.

Lamb koftas

Makes **10**

| **POINTS** values per recipe | **29½** | calories per serving | **155** |

A great recipe for a summer lunch – skewers of spicy lamb that can be cooked on the barbecue and served with a crunchy zero **POINTS** value salad. *Preparation time 15 minutes + 20 minutes chilling l Cooking time 12–15 minutes*

FOR THE KOFTAS
500 g (1 lb 2 oz) minced lamb
1 egg yolk
100 g (3½ oz) fresh white breadcrumbs
1 onion, chopped
1 tablespoon chopped fresh parsley
½ teaspoon ground cinnamon
1 teaspoon ground cumin
½ teaspoon chilli powder
1 teaspoon turmeric
½ teaspoon ground allspice

FOR THE SAUCE
150 g (5½ oz) low fat plain yogurt
juice of ½ lemon
1 tablespoon tahini paste
2 garlic cloves, crushed

1 Soak 10 wooden kebab skewers in water for at least 30 minutes.
2 Place all the kofta ingredients in a food processor and blend until completely mixed.
3 Using your hands, form the mixture into balls and squeeze on to the end of the skewers. Place on a plate or tray and cover with cling film. Leave to chill in the fridge for 20 minutes.
4 In a bowl, mix together the sauce ingredients and place in the fridge until ready to serve.
5 Heat the grill until quite hot and cook the koftas for about 12–15 minutes, turning quite often to prevent them from burning. If using a barbecue the same applies – keep checking them to prevent burning.
6 Serve with the tahini and yogurt sauce.

TOP TIP Soaking the kebab skewers prevents them from burning when the koftas are cooking.

Roasted vegetable open lasagne

Serves **2 V**

| **POINTS** values per recipe | **9** | calories per serving | **290** |

This is a cheat's version in which the lasagne does not need any baking! Roast the filling, quickly cook the fresh pasta and assemble. It really is that simple! *Preparation time 15 minutes l Cooking time 50 minutes*

4 garlic cloves, peeled

2 carrots, peeled and cut in chunks

4 shallots, peeled and halved

1 red and 1 yellow pepper, de-seeded and sliced

1 small aubergine, cut in chunks

low fat cooking spray

8 sage leaves

8 cherry tomatoes on the vine

4 sheets fresh lasagne

3 tablespoons green pesto

salt and freshly ground black pepper

basil leaves, to garnish

1 Preheat the oven to Gas Mark 7/220°C/fan oven 200°C. Place all the vegetables except the sage leaves and tomatoes in a roasting tin, large enough for them to be in one layer. Spray with the low fat cooking spray and roast for 30 minutes, tossing occasionally.

2 Add the sage leaves and tomatoes and roast for a further 20 minutes until the vegetables are lightly charred. Season.

3 Meanwhile, cut each lasagne sheet in half and put it in a large dish or pan. Cover the lasagne sheets with boiling water and soak for 5 minutes, then drain thoroughly.

4 On a plate, layer the lasagne and roasted vegetables, drizzling each layer with pesto. Serve the dish garnished with basil leaves.

TOP TIP Line the roasting tin with foil before using – it makes washing up a lot easier! Roast the vegetables the day before, then cool, cover and chill before reheating in the microwave when ready to use.

VARIATION Try a springtime roasted vegetable variation using the 4 garlic cloves, 110 g (4 oz) green beans, halved, 110 g (4 oz) asparagus spears, halved, six baby carrots and six spring onions, halved. The **POINTS** values will remain the same.

Coronation chicken and pasta salad

Serves **1**

| **POINTS** values per recipe | **5** | calories per serving | **290** |

This is a great way to use up cooked chicken, particularly from a roast, when it will have the most flavour. *Preparation and cooking time 15 minutes*

40 g (1½ oz) pasta shells
60 g (2 oz) baby sweetcorn, halved
125 g (4½ oz) cooked chicken breast, skin removed
2 tablespoons 0% fat Greek yogurt
1 teaspoon medium curry paste
½ red pepper, de-seeded and sliced
1 tablespoon coriander leaves, chopped
zest of ½ lemon, grated finely
2 spring onions cut in strips to garnish
salt and freshly ground black pepper

1 Bring a pan of water to the boil, add the pasta and cook for 10–12 minutes or according to the packet instructions, adding the baby sweetcorn for the final 5 minutes of cooking time. Drain and rinse in plenty of cold water.

2 Cut the chicken into strips or chunks and place in a large bowl. Mix together the yogurt and curry paste with 1 tablespoon of warm water and season.

3 Add the pasta, baby sweetcorn, red pepper, coriander leaves and lemon zest to the chicken, pour over the yogurt dressing and mix well. Serve sprinkled with spring onions.

TOP TIPS Fresh herbs have maximum flavour if chopped at the very last minute before using.

Summer fruit and white chocolate fool

Serves **2 V**

| **POINTS** values per recipe | **7** | calories per serving | **140** |

A light and delicious fool. The white chocolate is enough to sweeten the fool without having to add any sugar. *Preparation time 15 minutes + 30 minutes chilling*

300 g can of summer fruits, drained
25 g (1 oz) white cooking chocolate
100 g (3½ oz) very low fat plain fromage frais
50 g (1¾ oz) fresh raspberries, to decorate

1 Purée the summer fruits in a blender, then place in a large bowl.

2 Meanwhile, melt the white chocolate in a large heatproof bowl over a small saucepan of simmering water. Add to the fruit purée and blend again. Fold in the fromage frais and pour into serving glasses or bowls. Serve at once or chill and serve later. Decorate with fresh raspberries.

TOP TIP To melt chocolate, place a saucepan of water on the hob and bring to the boil. Reduce the heat until it is gently simmering. Cut the chocolate into chunks and place it in a heatproof bowl. Put the bowl over the saucepan of water so that the base does not touch the water. Let the chocolate melt gently.

Roasted fruits with orange sauce

Serves **4 V**

| **POINTS** values per recipe | 8 | calories per serving | 183 |

A delicious way to serve fruit – the roasting not only softens it but also draws out the flavours. *Preparation and cooking time 45 minutes*

200 g (7 oz) large strawberries, hulled
2 kiwi fruits, peeled and quartered
1 medium mango, peeled and sliced thickly
4 peaches, quartered
½ teaspoon ground cinnamon
juice and zest of 1 orange zest
4 passion fruit
200 g low fat plain yogurt, to serve

1 Preheat the oven to Gas Mark 7/220°C/fan oven 200°C.
2 Place the first four fruits into a bowl and sprinkle with the ground cinnamon and orange zest, then mix gently.
3 Pour the fruits into a roasting tray and roast for 30 minutes, turning them gently after 15 minutes.
4 Place the orange juice in a pan with the juice of the passion fruit – the pips can be sieved out if you wish but it is not necessary. Simmer on a medium heat for 15 minutes until the liquid has reduced slightly.
5 Serve the roasted fruits with the orange sauce and the low fat yogurt.

Apple snow

Serves **4 V**

| **POINTS** values per recipe | 4 | calories per serving | 98 |

A light and fluffy fruity dessert that's easy to prepare ahead – and the perfect recipe for using up those windfall apples. *Preparation time 20 minutes + chilling*

700 g (1 lb 9 oz) cooking apples, cored, peeled and chopped
½ teaspoon ground cinnamon
4 tablespoons granulated sweetener
100 g (3½ oz) low fat plain yogurt
1 egg white
1 dessert apple, cored and sliced

1 Place the cooking apples in a saucepan with the cinnamon and 2 tablespoons of water. Cover the pan and cook gently for 10 minutes, stirring occasionally, until the apples have softened to a purée. Transfer to a mixing bowl, stir in the sweetener and leave to cool.
2 Stir the yogurt into the cooled apple purée. Beat the egg white in a clean bowl until it holds soft peaks and then fold it into the apple mixture using a metal spoon. Divide between four dessert dishes, cover with clingfilm and chill for 1 hour.
3 Top the apple snow with the sliced apple before serving.

5 A DAY Apples contain vitaminutes and fibre and count towards your minimum of 5 portions of fruit and vegetables a day.

TOP TIP When beating egg whites always start your mixer on a low speed then gradually increase the speed once they are frothy. This creates many small bubbles rather than fewer large ones, giving a more stable structure, which is especially important when making meringue mixture.

Panna cotta

Serves **4**

| **POINTS** values per recipe | **19½** | calories per serving | **98** |

This rich and creamy Italian set custard is an easy and delicious dinner party dessert. Top it with caramelised orange sticks for an extra treat.
Preparation and cooking time 15 minutes + chilling time

425 ml (¾ pint) semi skimmed milk
126 g sachet Supercook vege gel or gelatine
110 g (4 oz) caster sugar
4 egg yolks, beaten
finely grated zest of 1 orange
2 tablespoons half fat crème fraîche

FOR THE TOPPING
strips of peel (see Top Tip) from 1 orange, plus the juice
   (4 tablespoons)
2 teaspoons sugar

1 Place 200 ml (7 fl oz) of the milk in bowl and sprinkle over the vege gel. Stir to dissolve and set aside. If using gelatine, warm the milk in a small pan to just below boiling point, remove from the heat, sprinkle over the gelatine and stir to dissolve.

2 Mix the remaining milk and sugar in a pan over a low heat, stirring to dissolve the sugar and bring to the boil. Add the egg yolks and, stirring continuously, bring back to the boil and cook for 1 minute until the mixture coats the back of the spoon. Add the dissolved vege gel mixture or gelatine and bring back to just below boiling point. Do not boil. Strain the mixture at this point if it is at all lumpy.

3 Stir in the orange zest and crème fraîche. Pour into 150 ml (5 fl oz) ramekins and leave to cool. They should set almost immediately, but chill for at least 1 hour before serving.

4 To make the topping, place the ingredients in a small pan, bring to the boil and simmer for 2–3 minutes until reduced and syrupy. Cool and serve on top of the panna cotta.

TOP TIP To make orange strips, use a vegetable peeler or knife to pare the rind, leaving the bitter white pith behind, then cut into thin sticks.

VARIATION Try other flavourings such as 1 teaspoon of vanilla extract, 1 teaspoon of finely grated nutmeg or 1 teaspoon of cinnamon.

Hot peppered pineapple

Serves **4**

| **POINTS** values per recipe | **6½** | calories per serving | **70** |

A deliciously different recipe – pineapple that is blanched with pepper and sugar syrup and then griddled and topped with creamy crème fraîche.
Preparation time 15 minutes l Cooking time 15 minutes + 30 minutes cooling time

1 medium pineapple, peeled, cored and cut into thick half moon slices
300 ml (½ pint) water
2 teaspoons artificial sweetener
¼ teaspoon freshly ground black pepper
75 g (2¾ oz) half fat crème fraîche

1 Place the pineapple slices in a medium saucepan with the water, sweetener and pepper. Bring to the boil and then simmer for 8–10 minutes until the pineapple is tender but not too soft.
2 Take the pan off the heat and leave the pineapple to cool in the syrup.
3 Heat a griddle pan until it is really hot and place the pineapple slices on it. Cook on both sides, briefly – just enough to colour and slightly char them.
4 Serve the pineapple with the low fat crème fraîche.

TOP TIP If you find that the pineapple is too hot, add slightly less pepper next time.

Pistachio ice cream

Serves **6** ❄

| **POINTS** values per recipe | **20½** | calories per serving | **140** |

This is a creamy ice cream that is delicately flavoured with pistachio nuts. It makes a great dinner party treat. *Preparation and cooking time 20 minutes + freezing time*

4 egg yolks
6 tablespoons caster sugar
1 teaspoon cornflour
600 ml (1 pint) semi skimmed milk
110 g (4 oz) pistachio nuts, chopped finely
1–2 drops of green colouring (optional)

1 In a large bowl whisk together the egg yolks, sugar and cornflour until pale and creamy.

2 Pour the milk into a medium sized pan, add the nuts and bring to the boil. Remove from the heat and whisk into the egg mixture. Return to the pan and cook over a low heat for 2–3 minutes until thickened; it should coat the back of the spoon. Stir in the green colouring, if using.

3 Pour into a freezer proof container and freeze for 2 hours or until semi solid. Remove from the freezer and mash, using a fork to break up large chunks of ice. Return to the freezer and freeze overnight.

4 Alternatively use an ice cream machine to churn the mixture, then serve immediately or freeze. To serve, remove from the freezer 20 minutes beforehand. Serve two medium sized scoops per person.

Potato pizza

Serves **2 V**

| **POINTS** values per recipe | **8½** | calories per serving | **395** |

This pizza is always a hot favourite at dinner parties. Serve in thin wedges as a starter.
Preparation time 5 minutes l Cooking time 15–20 minutes

250 g (9 oz) waxy potatoes, peeled, sliced thinly, rinsed and
   patted dry on kitchen paper
2 garlic cloves, crushed
leaves from 1 sprig of rosemary
low fat cooking spray
1 large, thin (30 cm/12 inch) fresh pizza base
1 teaspoon olive oil
plain flour, for dusting
salt and freshly ground black pepper

1 Preheat the oven to Gas Mark 7/220°C/fan oven 200°C. Put the potatoes, garlic, rosemary and seasoning in a bowl, spray with the low fat cooking spray, toss together then spray again.
2 Place the pizza base on an oven tray sprayed with the low fat cooking spray and dusted with a little flour.
3 Spread the potato mixture evenly over the pizza base, drizzle with olive oil and bake for 15–20 minutes until the potatoes are tender and the pizza lightly golden and crisp.

TOP TIP This is best made with waxy potato varieties, which include Desirée (the red-skinned potato) and new and early potatoes such as Pentland Javelin and Maris Pipper.

Cook ahead Deep South stew

Serves **1 V** ❄

| **POINTS** values per recipe | **3** | calories per serving | **253** |

A rich, warming stew based on the flavours popular in the southern states of America. Serve with fresh greens such as green beans or broccoli. *Preparation time 15 minutes l Cooking time 15–20 minutes*

low fat cooking spray
1 small onion, sliced finely
1 garlic clove, crushed
50 g (1¾ oz) baby carrots
50 g (1¾ oz) okra or green beans
50 g (1¾ oz) baby sweetcorn
1 tablespoon tomato purée
200 g can of chopped tomatoes
½ teaspoon dried chilli flakes
½ teaspoon ground cinnamon
200 g can of kidney beans, drained and rinsed
200 ml (7 fl oz) vegetable stock
salt and freshly ground black pepper

1 Spray a large saucepan with the low fat cooking spray and fry the onion and garlic for 5 minutes, adding a little water if they stick, until softened. Add the carrots, okra or green beans, baby sweetcorn, tomato purée, tomatoes, spices, kidney beans, stock and seasoning.
2 Bring to the boil and then simmer gently with a lid on for 15–20 minutes or until all the vegetables are tender and the sauce is rich and thick.

For one and two

French ham and bean casserole

Serves **1**

| **POINTS** values per recipe | **4** | calories per serving | **327** |

This is a quick and satisfying stew for a cold night. Serve with spinach and mashed potatoes.
Preparation and cooking time 25 minutes

low fat cooking spray
1 small onion, chopped finely
1 garlic clove, crushed
200 g (7 oz) canned chopped tomatoes
1 teaspoon tomato purée
2 fresh thyme sprigs, woody stems discarded and leaves chopped
½ teaspoon dried oregano or Mediterranean herbs
1 celery stick, sliced finely
1 bay leaf
50 g (1¾ oz) thickly sliced lean ham, cubed
200 g (7 oz) canned haricot beans, drained
a small bunch of fresh parsley, chopped
salt and freshly ground black pepper

1 Spray a frying pan with the low fat cooking spray and fry the onion and garlic for 3 minutes, until softened, adding a tablespoon of water, if necessary, to prevent them from sticking.
2 Add the tomatoes and tomato purée, thyme, oregano or Mediterranean herbs, celery and bay leaf and bring to the boil. Season and simmer for 5 minutes until thick.
3 Add the ham and beans and simmer for a further 5 minutes. Stir through the parsley and then serve.

TOP TIP To mash potatoes, using a potato peeler, peel some floury potatoes such as King Edwards. Cut the potatoes into small chunks and put them in a saucepan. Cover with cold water. Bring the potatoes to the boil, cover and cook for 25 minutes or until they are tender. Remove any scum on the surface of the water, then drain. Add a few tablespoons of skimmed milk and mash together.

Fish'n'chips for one

Serves **1** ❄

| **POINTS** values per recipe | **7½** | calories per serving | **455** |

When you fancy fish and chips but don't want to use too many **POINTS** values, this recipe is ideal.
Preparation and cooking time 40 minutes

175 g (6 oz) potatoes, cut into thin sticks
1 tablespoon sunflower oil
½ teaspoon salt
1 x 175 g (6 oz) cod loin
1 teaspoon plain white flour
1 egg white
25 g (1 oz) fresh white breadcrumbs
low fat cooking spray
lemon wedge, to garnish

1 Preheat the oven to Gas Mark 6/200°C/fan oven 180°C.

2 Rinse the potato sticks to remove the excess starch and pat dry with kitchen paper. Place in a plastic container with a tight fitting lid. Add the oil and salt. Place the lid on the container and shake thoroughly so all the potatoes get a thin coating of salty oil.

3 Spread the chips out on a non stick baking sheet and bake for 20–25 minutes, until they are golden and crispy.

4 Meanwhile, rinse the cod loin and pat dry with kitchen paper, and then dust it with the flour.

5 Whisk the egg white until it becomes foamy. Dip the fish into the egg white and then coat it in the breadcrumbs. Lightly spray the crumbed fish with low fat cooking spray and then place it on a non stick baking tray.

6 Bake the fish for 15–20 minutes, until it is cooked through and the crumb coating is golden and crunchy.

7 Serve the fish and chips on a warmed serving plate and garnish with a wedge of lemon.

TIP Preheat the baking tray for 5 minutes before putting the fish on to it, to make the fish crispy underneath.

Spanish meatballs

Serves **2** ❄

| **POINTS** values per recipe | **12½** | calories per serving | **420** |

These little meatballs are dry fried and cooked in tomato sauce for an easy meal with a Spanish flavour. *Preparation time 15 minutes l Cooking time 25 minutes*

150 g (5½ oz) lean minced lamb
1 small onion, chopped finely
1 garlic clove, crushed
2 teaspoons mixed dried herbs
1 small egg white, beaten lightly
2 tablespoons brandy
100 g (3½ oz) button mushrooms, sliced
300 ml (10 fl oz) passata
1 tablespoon tomato purée
1 teaspoon paprika
1 vegetable stock cube, dissolved in 150 ml (5 fl oz) boiling water
100 g (3½ oz) spaghetti or other pasta shapes
salt and freshly ground black pepper
chopped fresh parsley, to garnish

1 In a mixing bowl, combine the minced lamb, onion, garlic, dried herbs and egg white and season. Using clean hands, form the mixture into small meatballs.

2 Heat a large non stick frying pan and add the meatballs, dry frying them until they are lightly browned. Pour in the brandy and let it bubble up for a few moments, and then add the mushrooms, passata, tomato purée, paprika and stock. Heat until simmering, and then cook gently for 20–25 minutes to reduce the liquid by about one third, stirring occasionally.

3 10 minutes before the end of the cooking time, cook the pasta in plenty of boiling water according to the packet instructions until just tender. Drain thoroughly.

4 Divide the pasta between two warmed plates and top with the meatballs and sauce. Garnish with plenty of parsley.

Thai steamed salmon

Serves **2**

| **POINTS** values per recipe | **12½** | calories per serving | **310** |

Steaming times for fish are totally dependent on the thickness rather than the weight, so measure your fish carefully. This Thai-influenced recipe is light yet flavoursome. *Preparation and cooking time 30 minutes*

low fat cooking spray
4 medium shallots, sliced finely
2.5 cm (1 inch) piece of fresh root ginger, sliced into fine matchsticks
2 garlic cloves, sliced into fine slivers
25 g (1 oz) soft brown sugar
2 tablespoons fish sauce
2 salmon steaks, each about 3 cm (1¼ inch) thick and weighing approximately 150 g (5½ oz) each
fresh coriander, to garnish

1 Heat a frying pan and spray with the low fat cooking spray. Fry the shallots, ginger and garlic for 1 minute until aromatic, then add the sugar and fish sauce. Stir then set aside.
2 Place each piece of salmon on the middle of a piece of baking paper, at least 4 times its size. Pile the ginger mixture on top of each and then fold up the baking paper around the fish to make an air tight parcel.
3 Place both parcels in a steamer, cover and steam for 10 minutes or until the steaks are opaque and cooked through. Serve immediately with the juices poured over and fresh coriander sprigs.

TOP TIPS Steam fish either in a fish kettle, bamboo steamer or a saucepan with a steaming basket.

Hot peppered chicken salad

Serves **2**

| **POINTS** values per recipe | **5½** | calories per serving | **200** |

The contrasting colours of the red skinned apples and the deep green spinach make this a very attractive and appetising dish. *Preparation time 15 minutes l Cooking time 20 minutes*

2 x 125 g (4½ oz) skinless chicken breasts
1 tablespoon freshly ground mixed pepper
low fat cooking spray
1 red skinned dessert apple (e.g. Braeburn)
1 tablespoon fresh lemon juice
175 g (6 oz) baby spinach leaves
3 tablespoons low fat plain yogurt
1 tablespoon finely chopped fresh chives

1 Preheat the oven to Gas Mark 6/200°C/fan oven 180°C. Line a baking sheet with non stick baking parchment.
2 Season the chicken breasts generously with the mixed pepper and spray them lightly with low fat cooking spray. Place the chicken on the prepared baking sheet and roast it for 20 minutes.
3 Core the apple and slice it thinly. Toss it together with the lemon juice and baby spinach leaves and divide the mixture between two plates.
4 Mix the yogurt with the chives. Slice each chicken breast on the slant – each breast should give 5–6 slices. Pile the slices randomly on top of the spinach and apple. Drizzle with the yogurt and chive dressing, and serve.

TOP TIP Add the chicken while it is still warm, this way it begins to just wilt the spinach.

Steak and ale pie

Serves **1**

| **POINTS** values per recipe | **7** | calories per serving | **403** |

Preparation time 25 minutes l Cooking time 50–55 minutes

low fat cooking spray
1 small onion, chopped finely
1 carrot, chopped finely
1 celery stick, chopped finely
1 fresh sage sprig, chopped (optional)
100 ml (3½ fl oz) chicken stock
100 g (3½ oz) mushrooms
75 g (2¾ oz) lean sirloin steak, fat removed and meat cubed
1 teaspoon flour
2 tablespoons ale
salt and freshly ground black pepper

FOR THE PASTRY
50 g (1¾ oz) ready rolled puff pastry
1 teaspoon skimmed milk, to glaze

1 Heat a non stick saucepan and spray with the low fat cooking spray. Fry the onion, carrot, celery and sage (if using) for 5 minutes or until softened, adding a little stock if necessary to prevent them from sticking.

2 Add the mushrooms, season and stir fry for a further 2 minutes; then remove all the vegetables to a plate.

3 Spray the pan again, season and fry the meat until browned all over; then sprinkle with the flour, return the vegetables to the pan and stir it all together.

4 Pour over the remaining stock and ale and bring to the boil. Reduce the heat, cover and simmer for 30 minutes on a low heat.

5 Meanwhile, roll out the puff pastry to fit an individual pie dish. Preheat the oven to Gas Mark 4/180°C/fan oven 160°C. Spoon the cooked filling into the dish and lay the pastry on top, pressing down at the edges.

6 Brush with a little skimmed milk and cut a slit in the middle. Bake for 20–25 minutes or until golden.

Pesto, Quorn and pepper kebabs

Serves **2 V** ❄

| **POINTS** values per recipe | **6** | calories per serving | **280** |

Preparation and cooking time 20 minutes

225 g (8 oz) Quorn pieces
2 tablespoons pesto
1 red pepper, de-seeded and cut into squares
1 green pepper, de-seeded and cut into squares
1 yellow pepper, de-seeded and cut into squares
2 small red onions, cut into thick wedges
8 bay leaves

1 Place the Quorn pieces in a bowl with the pesto and mix well.
2 Thread the pesto coated Quorn pieces on to 4 skewers alternating with squares of pepper, red onion wedges and bay leaves.
3 Grill for 8–10 minutes, turning frequently, until the vegetables begin to char around the edges. Serve 2 kebabs per person.

Mushroom frittata

Serves **1 V**

| **POINTS** values per recipe | **1½** | calories per serving | **142** |

Preparation and cooking time 25 minutes

low fat cooking spray
1 garlic clove, chopped finely
250 g (9 oz) mushrooms, sliced
1 lemon wedge
1 egg
1 egg white
a few sprigs of parsley or thyme, chopped
salt and freshly ground black pepper

1 Heat a small non stick frying pan and spray with the low fat cooking spray, then stir fry the garlic for a minute until golden. With the heat on high add the mushrooms and stir fry for a minute. Season, then squeeze the lemon wedge over them.
2 Beat the egg and egg white together with the parsley or thyme in a small bowl until frothy. Then turn down the heat and add to the mushrooms. Cook for 1–2 minutes until the base of the omelette has set.
3 Preheat the grill to High, brown the top and then cut into wedges to serve.

TOP TIP To separate an egg, crack a fresh one on the side of the bowl and break the egg shell into two halves, using your thumbs to pull it apart. Over a bowl, gently rock the yolk back and forth between the two halves of shell, allowing the white to slip into the bowl. Continue doing this until the white is out, then place the yolk in a separate bowl.

Lamb stuffed red peppers

Serves **2**

| **POINTS** values per recipe | **8½** | calories per serving | **285** |

Serve with a zero **POINTS** value green vegetable such as broccoli and 100 g (3½ oz) new potatoes for 1 extra **POINTS** value. *Preparation time 10 minutes l Cooking time 35–45 minutes*

2 large red peppers
low fat cooking spray
1 small onion, chopped
1 teaspoon peeled and chopped fresh root ginger
1 garlic clove, crushed
½ teaspoon garam masala
200 g (7 oz) minced lamb
½ green chilli, de-seeded and chopped finely
1 tablespoon chopped fresh coriander
salt and freshly ground black pepper

1 Preheat the oven to Gas Mark 4/180°C/fan oven 160°C. Halve the peppers, cutting through the stalk. Scoop out the seeds.
2 Spray an ovenproof dish with low fat cooking spray and place the peppers in the dish.
3 Spray a frying pan with low fat cooking spray and fry the onion until golden.
4 Lower the heat and add the ginger, garlic, seasoning and garam masala. Stir fry for 2–3 minutes.
5 Add the minced lamb and fry for about 10–12 minutes. Add the green chilli and chopped fresh coriander and stir fry for another 2–3 minutes.
6 Spoon the lamb mixture into the red peppers. Bake for 15–20 minutes. Serve immediately.

TOP TIP Always wash your hands and the knife you have been using after chopping chillies, and be careful not to touch your eyes until you have done this – it will burn!

VARIATION Other coloured peppers or large beefsteak tomatoes could also be used in this recipe – make the filling in the same way and stuff the vegetables before placing in the oven. Tomatoes will take slightly less time to cook. The **POINTS** values will remain the same.

VEGETARIAN OPTION, mix 150 g (5½ oz) cooked couscous with a 5 cm (2 inch) piece of cucumber, finely chopped, 2 tomatoes, finely chopped and 1 tablespoon of chopped fresh coriander. Use to fill the peppers in step 6. The **POINTS** value will be reduced to 1 per serving.

Jamaican potato and beans

Serves **2 V**

| **POINTS** values per recipe | **11½** | calories per serving | **375** |

This thick, earthy stew is made by combining delicious flavours that bring sunny Jamaica a little closer during the winter months. *Preparation time 25 minutes l Cooking time 30 minutes*

600 ml (1 pint) stock or water
100 ml (3½ fl oz) reduced fat coconut milk
2 medium carrots, cut into 2.5 cm (1 inch) sticks
1 medium green pepper, de-seeded and sliced
1 medium onion, chopped finely
1 medium potato, peeled and diced
1 bay leaf
2 sprigs thyme
2 garlic cloves, chopped
1 chilli pepper, de-seeded and chopped
1 medium sweet potato, diced
1 medium parsnip, cubed
400 g can kidney beans, drained
1 tablespoon soy sauce
salt and freshly ground black pepper

1 Bring the stock or water and coconut milk to the boil in a large saucepan and simmer for 5 minutes. Add the carrots, pepper and onion. Simmer for 10 minutes.

2 Add the potato, bay leaf, thyme, garlic and chilli. Simmer for a further 10 minutes then add the sweet potato and parsnip and simmer for 20 minutes more.

3 When all the vegetables are almost done, add the beans, soy and seasoning and stir well before serving.

VARIATIONS The beans and vegetables can be varied to include whatever zero **POINTS** values vegetables you have available.

Fresh tomato and feta pasta

Serves **1 V**

| **POINTS** values per recipe | **6** | calories per serving | **399** |

A fresh tasting pasta dish that combines all the flavours of the Mediterranean summer. *Preparation and cooking time 20 minutes*

200 g (7 oz) small tomatoes on the vine
4 garlic cloves, unpeeled
60 g (2 oz) dried tagliatelle
2 teaspoons balsamic vinegar
1 teaspoon olive oil
½ teaspoon sugar
25 g (1 oz) feta cheese, cubed
a small bunch of fresh basil, torn
salt and freshly ground black pepper

1 Preheat the oven to Gas Mark 7/220°C/fan oven 200°C and place the tomatoes and garlic on a baking tray. Season and roast for 10–15 minutes.

2 Meanwhile, cook the pasta in plenty of boiling water for 10–15 minutes, or according to the pack instructions and then drain and return to the saucepan.

3 Add the roasted tomatoes, removing and discarding the vine.

4 Squeeze the garlic out of the skins and chop the flesh, then add to the pasta with the balsamic vinegar, olive oil, sugar, feta cheese, basil and seasoning. Toss together and serve immediately.

Banana split

Serves **1 V**

| **POINTS** values per recipe | **3** | calories per serving | **250** |

A quick and easy sweet treat for you to enjoy.
Preparation time 5 minutes

1 small banana, peeled and split lengthways
60 g (2 oz) scoop low fat ice cream
150 g (5½ oz) fresh strawberries, rinsed, drained and hulled
1 teaspoon icing sugar

1 Arrange the banana halves in a sundae boat or on a plate then divide the ice cream between them.
2 Halve the strawberries and scatter over the ice cream, sprinkle with sugar and serve.

Quick pineapple trifle

Serves **1 V**

| **POINTS** values per recipe | **3½** | calories per serving | **280** |

This easy recipe is just the thing when you fancy a low **POINTS** value treat just for yourself. *Preparation and cooking time 15 minutes*

2 sponge fingers, crumbled
¼ of 227 g can of pineapple chunks in natural juice
125 g tub of low fat custard

1 Place the sponge finger crumbs in the base of an individual dish.
2 Spoon the pineapple (reserving two chunks) and any juice over the crumbs. Leave the dish to stand for 5–10 minutes, so the sponge absorbs the juice.
3 Top with the custard and then decorate with the reserved pineapple. Chill in the fridge until required.

Baked nectarines, ricotta and amaretti

Serves **2 V** ❄

| **POINTS** values per recipe | **6½** | calories per serving | **205** |

Preparation time 15 minutes l Baking time 15 minutes

2 nectarines, halved and stoned
50 g (1¾ oz) ricotta cheese
1 teaspoon clear honey
25 g (1 oz) amaretti biscuits, crushed
1 tablespoon amaretto liqueur

1 Preheat the oven to Gas Mark 4/180°C/fan oven 160°C. Place the nectarines, cut halves facing up, on a baking tray.
2 Beat together the ricotta cheese, honey, amaretti biscuits and Amaretto liqueur.
3 Spoon the cheese mixture on top of the nectarine halves, pressing down slightly.
4 Bake the nectarines for 15 minutes. Serve hot.

TOP TIP Cut a small slice off the base of each nectarine to stop them wobbling on the baking tray.

Eton mess

Serves **2 V**

| **POINTS** values per recipe | **2½** | calories per serving | **75** |

A fantastically, simple recipe – sweet and satisfying and just 1 **POINTS** value! *Preparation time 5 minutes*

1 meringue nest
100 ml (3½ fl oz) very low fat plain yogurt
150 g (5½ oz) fresh strawberries, sliced or chopped
2 passion fruits

1 Break up the meringue nest in a medium bowl.
2 Add the yogurt and strawberries and mix very gently.
3 Divide the mixture between two glasses.
4 Cut the passion fruit in half and scrape out the flesh. Strain the flesh through a sieve and pour the juice over the glasses of Eton mess. Serve immediately.

VARIATION Most fruits can be used for this recipe although summer fruits tend to work best. Try using 125 g (4½ oz) raspberries instead of the strawberries. The **POINTS** values will remain the same. If you want to make a creamier version, try using 0% fat Greek yogurt instead. The **POINTS** values will remain the same.

Plum crumble

| **POINTS** values per recipe | **6** | calories per serving | **355** |

The crumble topping for this fruity pudding is quickly made by mixing muesli into melted margarine. You then mix in a little grated marzipan. *Preparation time 10 minutes l Cooking time 25–30 minutes*

2 plums, stoned and sliced
1 tablespoon light muscovado sugar
2 teaspoons polyunsaturated margarine
2 tablespoons no sugar muesli
15 g (½ oz) marzipan, grated

TO SERVE
2 tablespoons plain low fat yogurt
a pinch of ground cinnamon (optional)

1 Preheat the oven to Gas Mark 5/190°C/fan oven 170°C.
2 Put the plums in an individual baking dish and scatter half the sugar over them. Bake for 5 minutes while preparing the topping.
3 Melt the margarine in a saucepan, remove from the heat and stir in the muesli, the remaining sugar and the marzipan. Sprinkle the topping over the plums in an even layer.
4 Bake for about 20–25 minutes, until the plums are tender and the topping is crunchy and golden brown.
5 Serve with the yogurt, sprinkled with a little ground cinnamon, if you like.

VARIATIONS This recipe works well with baking apples. Rhubarb could also be used – you may need to add some powdered sweetener, as it can be quite tart. The marzipan tastes wonderful, but if you don't like it, or you want to reduce the **POINTS** values, simply leave it out and deduct 1 **POINTS** value.

Tropical mango creams

Serves **2 V** *if using vegetarian cheese and vegetarian fromage frais*

| **POINTS** values per recipe | **3½** | calories per serving | **145** |

A simple recipe that takes only a little more effort than an instant whip to make, contains far less **POINTS** values and is delicious. *Preparation time 5 minutes + chilling*

210 g can mango pieces in juice, drained
100 g (3½ oz) Quark cheese
pared zest and juice of 1 lime
4 tablespoons virtually fat free fromage frais

1 Purée the mango in a food processor then beat into the Quark, lime juice and fromage frais. Spoon into serving dishes and decorate with pared lime zest.
2 Chill then serve.

VARIATION Replace the mango with canned papaya in light syrup.

Pear bruschetta

Serves **2 V**

| **POINTS** values per recipe | **4** | calories per serving | **120** |

Serve with low fat custard. *Preparation and cooking time 15 minutes*

2 x 25 g (1 oz) slices of malt bread
227 g can of pear halves in natural juice, drained and juice reserved
½ teaspoon caster sugar
½ teaspoon chopped nuts or flaked almonds
1 teaspoon cornflour
a big pinch of ground cinnamon

1 Lightly toast the bread under a preheated medium grill on one side.
2 Slice the pear halves and then arrange in a fan-like shape on the untoasted side of each slice of bread. Sprinkle on half the sugar and all of the nuts. Grill under a medium heat until the sugar becomes lightly caramelised and the nuts turn golden.
3 Meanwhile blend the cornflour with a drop of the reserved juice, then stir in the remaining juice. Bring to the boil (either in a small saucepan or a jug in the microwave) until smooth and thickened. Stir in the remaining sugar and the cinnamon.
4 Drizzle the warm syrup over the grilled toasts. Serve immediately.

VARIATION Fresh ripe dessert pears can be used instead of canned. However, omit the cinnamon syrup and serve with 2 tablespoons of low fat plain yogurt, sprinkled with cinnamon.

Speedy coq au vin

Serves **4** ❄

| **POINTS** values per recipe | **14½** | calories per serving | **220** |

Serve with mashed potato and green beans (French, of course!), adding the extra **POINTS** values as necessary. *Preparation time 10 minutes l Cooking time 15 minutes*

6 shallots, halved
450 g (1 lb) boneless chicken breast, cubed
100 g (3½ oz) lean smoked bacon, diced
200 g (7 oz) button mushrooms
425 ml (¾ pint) hot chicken stock
150 ml (¼ pint) full-bodied dry red wine
2 teaspoons Worcestershire sauce
1 tablespoon chopped fresh thyme (or 1 teaspoon dried)
salt and freshly ground black pepper
a few thyme sprigs, to garnish

1 Pour some boiling water over the shallots, to cover, and leave for 5 minutes. This makes them very easy to peel – and without tears! Meanwhile, dry fry the chicken and the bacon in a non stick saucepan for 3 minutes, stirring frequently.
2 Add the mushrooms and the shallots to the chicken, together with a couple of tablespoons of stock. Cook briskly for 2 minutes, then reduce the heat and pour on the remaining stock and wine.
3 Stir in the Worcestershire sauce, thyme and a little seasoning, to taste. Cover and simmer for 15 minutes. Garnish with thyme sprigs and serve.

Chilli crab noodles

Serves **2**

| **POINTS** values per recipe | **12½** | calories per serving | **455** |

When time is of the essence, create this tasty dish from start to finish in just 20 minutes. *Preparation and cooking time 20 minutes*

150 g (5½ oz) vermicelli noodles
2 teaspoons sunflower oil
1 small red pepper, de-seeded and sliced thinly
100 g (3½ oz) baby sweetcorn, halved
6 spring onions, sliced
200 g (7 oz) canned white crab meat, drained
2 tablespoons sweet chilli sauce
2 tablespoons tomato ketchup
1 tablespoon soy sauce
2 tablespoons chopped fresh coriander, to serve

1 Place the noodles in a bowl and cover them with boiling water. Leave them to stand for 5 minutes and then drain thoroughly.
2 Meanwhile, heat the oil in a pan and stir fry the red pepper and baby sweetcorn for 2–3 minutes. Add the drained noodles, spring onions, crab meat, sweet chilli sauce, tomato ketchup and soy sauce, and stir fry for 2–3 minutes.
3 Scatter over the chopped fresh coriander and serve.

TOP TIPS Vermicelli noodles can go very soggy if left standing around for too long, so serve this dish immediately and avoid over soaking the noodles – 5 minutes is plenty of time as they are thinner than ordinary noodles.

Canned crab meat comes wrapped in paper; to drain it remove it from the can and squeeze the excess liquid out gently. Don't squeeze too much or you'll be left with very dry flakes.

Quick, slow

Chilli crusted lamb cutlets

Serves **4**

| **POINTS** values per recipe | **41½** | calories per serving | **505** |

Preparation and cooking time 25 minutes

3 large red chillies, de-seeded and chopped
2 spring onions, chopped
3 tablespoons lemon juice
2 tablespoons chopped fresh coriander
8 lamb cutlets
salt and freshly ground black pepper

FOR THE RAITA
¼ cucumber, grated
200 g (7 oz) low fat natural yogurt
1 chopped fresh tablespoon mint

1 Preheat the grill. Process the chillies, spring onions, lemon juice and coriander in a food processor until chopped roughly.
2 Spread the mixture over both sides of the cutlets. Season well. Place the cutlets on a baking tray and cook under a hot grill for 3–4 minutes on each side or until cooked to your liking.
3 Mix the raita ingredients together and serve with the cutlets.

Chinese pork parcels

Serves **4**

| **POINTS** values per recipe | **20** | calories per serving | **315** |

Try this nifty way with minced pork for an economical mid week meal. *Preparation and cooking time 20 minutes*

100 g (3½ oz) easy cook rice

450 g (1 lb) minced pork

2 fresh garlic cloves, chopped or 2 teaspoons garlic purée

1–2 teaspoons puréed ginger

2 tablespoons soy sauce

4 spring onions, trimmed and chopped

200 g bag of beansprouts

1 large carrot, grated

1 iceberg lettuce, whole leaves separated, to serve

freshly ground black pepper

1 Cook the rice according to pack instructions.

2 Dry fry the minced pork in a large frying pan for 5 minutes until lightly coloured and crumbly. Stir in the garlic and ginger and cook for a further 5 minutes to ensure the pork is well done.

3 Stir in the soy sauce, spring onions, beansprouts, carrot and pepper. Cook for 2–3 minutes.

4 Drain the rice, and stir into the pork. Arrange two whole lettuce leaves on each plate. Divide the mince mixture between them, roll each leaf up and enjoy with additional soy sauce, for dipping.

Warm potato and mackerel salad

Serves **2**

| **POINTS** values per recipe | **13** | calories per serving | **490** |

Salads served warm or at the very least, at room temperature, are more flavoursome than when eaten chilled. Try this salad and see! *Preparation and cooking time 25 minutes*

250 g (9 oz) new potatoes, quartered
200 g (7 oz) French beans, trimmed
½ red onion, sliced into rings
1 celery stick, chopped finely
4 cocktail gherkins in vinegar, drained and halved lengthways
2 teaspoons grated horseradish
150 ml (5 fl oz) 0% fat Greek yogurt
150 g (5½ oz) smoked mackerel fillets, flaked into large pieces
8 cherry tomatoes, whole, or 2 large tomatoes, quartered
salt and freshly ground black pepper
iceberg salad leaves, to serve

1 Cook the potatoes in boiling water for 10–15 minutes, or until tender and 5 minutes before the end, add the green beans. Drain and toss in the onion, celery and gherkins.
2 Mix the grated horseradish into the yogurt, and fold into the potato mixture. Season.
3 Arrange the mackerel and tomatoes on a bed of crisp salad leaves. Spoon over the warm potato salad and serve.

TOP TIP Make sure you don't use a creamed horseradish, which has a higher fat content.

VARIATION Replace the mackerel with 150 g (5½ oz) canned tuna in brine, drained. The **POINTS** value per serving will be 1.

Fusilli and chorizo sausage

Serves **1**

| **POINTS** values per recipe | **3½** | calories per serving | **220** |

Chorizo is a slightly spicy Spanish sausage that is available in most supermarkets now. Its lovely red colour comes from the paprika used to flavour it. *Preparation and cooking time 30 minutes*

40 g (1½ oz) fusilli
low fat cooking spray
½ onion, peeled and sliced
½ green pepper, seeded and sliced
25 g (1 oz) chorizo sausage, sliced
2 pepperdew piquante peppers (see Top Tip), drained and halved
salt and freshly ground black pepper
1 tablespoon parsley, chopped, to garnish

1 Bring a large pan of salted water to the boil, add the pasta and cook for 10–12 minutes or according to the packet instructions. Drain and rinse with boiling water.
2 Spray a frying pan with low fat cooking spray and heat until sizzling. Add the onion and green pepper and stir fry over a medium heat for 5 minutes until softened. Add the chorizo and continue frying for 2–3 minutes until the sausage is browned.
3 Toss in the pepperdew peppers and pasta and heat for 1 minute until the mixture is heated through. Season with salt and pepper and serve garnished with the chopped parsley.

TOP TIP Pepperdew peppers are sweet and spicy pickled peppers from South Africa. They are available in jars in most supermarkets, but if you can't find them substitute one canned pimiento. The **POINTS** values will remain the same.

VEGETARIAN OPTION Use 30 g (1¼ oz) chopped vegetarian sausage, which will make the **POINTS** values 3 per serving.

Squash and blue cheese risotto

Serves **2 V**

| **POINTS** values per recipe | **20** | calories per serving | **695** |

An interesting array of squashes have been appearing in the supermarkets and farmers' markets over the last couple of years, and are becoming more fashionable to cook with. This is the ideal recipe for those of you who have yet to try this interesting vegetable. *Preparation and cooking time 30 minutes*

2 teaspoons olive oil

1 large onion, chopped

2 celery sticks, chopped

450 g (1 lb) winter squash or pumpkin, skinned, de-seeded and cut into 1 cm (½ inch) cubes

200 g (7 oz) Italian style easy cook rice or Arborio rice

600 ml (1 pint) hot vegetable or chicken stock

4 sage leaves, torn or ½ teaspoon dried

2 tomatoes, de-seeded and diced

75 g (2¾ oz) low fat soft cheese with garlic and herbs

a handful of chopped fresh parsley

50 g (1¾ oz) blue cheese, crumbled

salt and freshly ground black pepper

1 Heat the oil in a large saucepan, and gently cook the onion and celery until softened. Add the squash or pumpkin and cook for 2 more minutes.

2 Stir in the rice and add the hot stock. Cover and simmer for 10–15 minutes, until the stock is nearly absorbed.

3 Stir in the sage, tomatoes, soft cheese and parsley. Season, to taste. Divide between the individual bowls, and crumble over the blue cheese.

TOP TIP'S Arborio rice is the classic short stubby grain used to give risotto its creamy consistency. It does, however, require more cooking than the easy cook Italian style rice, which is an acceptable 'cheats' version.

Omit the oil and dry fry the vegetables to save 1 **POINTS** value per serving. Replace the low fat soft cheese with virtually fat free fromage frais and save 1 **POINTS** value per serving.

Stilton, garlic and mushroom pizza

Serves **2 V**

| **POINTS** values per recipe | **9½** | calories per serving | **220** |

A creamy onion base topped with garlic mushrooms and oozing with blue cheese – delicious! *Preparation time 25 minutes l Cooking time 12 minutes*

low fat cooking spray
2 red onions, peeled and sliced in rings
23 cm (9 inch) ready made thin and crispy pizza base
250 g (9 oz) button mushrooms, halved
2 cloves garlic, peeled and crushed
2 tablespoons thyme leaves or 1 tablespoon dried thyme
40 g (1½ oz) Stilton, crumbled

1 Spray a frying pan with low fat cooking spray and when it is hot, add the onions and cook over a medium heat for 10 minutes, stirring occasionally until softened and lightly browned.
2 Spray a baking sheet with low fat cooking spray. Place the pizza base on the baking sheet and top with the onion rings.
3 Respray the frying pan with low fat cooking spray and heat until sizzling. Add the mushrooms and cook over a medium heat for 5 minutes until the juices begin to flow. Add the garlic and thyme and continue cooking for 3–4 minutes until the juices have evaporated.
4 Meanwhile, preheat the oven to Gas mark 7/220°C/fan oven 200°C. Spread the mushrooms over the onions and top with the cheese. Bake the pizza for 12–15 minutes until golden and bubbling.

TOP TIP Adding the garlic after cooking the mushrooms for 5 minutes stops it from burning and becoming bitter.

Lazy lamb and lentils

Serves **4 V** ❄

| **POINTS** values per recipe | **13½** | calories per serving | **260** |

We've called this dish 'lazy' since it needs so little preparation or attention. *Preparation time 10 minutes l Cooking time 20 minutes*

350 g (12 oz) lean lamb, cut into 2 cm (¾ inch) pieces
1 onion, chopped
2 teaspoons garlic purée
2 teaspoons harissa (e.g. Bart's)
100 g (3½ oz) red lentils
200 g canned, chopped tomatoes
300 ml (½ pint) hot lamb or chicken stock
2 tablespoons chopped fresh parsley
salt and freshly ground black pepper

1 Dry fry the lamb in a non stick pan for 5 minutes, until lightly browned all over.
2 Add the onion, garlic and the harissa and continue to cook for a further 3–4 minutes. Add the lentils, tomatoes and stock. Bring to the boil, then cover and simmer for 20 minutes, or until the lentils are tender and the stock is nearly all absorbed.
3 Stir in the parsley. Check the seasoning, to taste. Serve.

TOP TIP Lentils are a great source of protein and can be used in place of some of the meat in recipes. They are also delicious in soups so it's a good idea to keep a packet of red lentils, which don't need pre-soaking of course, in your store cupboard.

Red hot pepper pasta

Serves **4 V**

| **POINTS** values per recipe | **22** | calories per serving | **386** |

This pasta dish with a kick is great as an after work supper or for lunch with friends. *Preparation and cooking time 30 minutes*

250 g (9 oz) spinach, tomato or plain dried pasta shapes
200 g (7 oz) watercress, chopped coarsely
100 g (3½ oz) feta cheese, crumbled
1 tablespoon pine nut kernels, toasted
salt and freshly ground black pepper

FOR THE SAUCE
4 red peppers, halved and de-seeded
2 garlic cloves, crushed
2 tablespoons balsamic vinegar
1–2 small red chillies, de-seeded and chopped finely

1 Cook the pasta as instructed on the pack, until al dente. Preheat the grill to a high heat.
2 Meanwhile, to make the sauce, grill the red peppers skin side up until blistered and blackened. Place in a plastic bag and leave until cool enough to handle.
3 Peel off the charred skin and place the flesh in a liquidiser with the other sauce ingredients. Add a few tablespoons or enough water to enable you to process to a smooth purée.
4 Drain the pasta and return to the pan. Immediately add the remaining ingredients. Toss, then serve.

Polenta with garlic mushrooms

Serves **4 V**

| **POINTS** values per recipe | **20½** | calories per serving | **355** |

Polenta makes an interesting alternative to rice and pasta. *Preparation and cooking time 40 minutes + 30 minutes setting*

2 vegetable stock cubes, crumbled
350 g (12 oz) polenta
2 tablespoons finely chopped fresh chives
25 g (1 oz) Parmesan cheese, grated
low fat cooking spray
450 g (1 lb) open cup mushrooms, halved
2 garlic cloves, chopped finely
salt and freshly ground black pepper
1 tablespoon chopped fresh parsley, to garnish

1 In a large saucepan, bring 850 ml (1½ pints) water and the crumbled stock cubes to a fast boil. Add the polenta and beat well. Reduce the heat and simmer for 5 minutes, stirring continuously.

2 Remove the pan from the heat and beat in the chives and Parmesan cheese. Pour the polenta mixture into a 18 cm x 23 cm (7 inch x 9 inch) shallow non stick square tin and allow it to set in the fridge for about 30 minutes.

3 When the polenta is firm to the touch, turn it out on to a clean board or work surface. Cut it into eight triangles and spray the pieces with low fat cooking spray. Cook them on a griddle pan for 2–3 minutes each side until they are warmed through and light brown.

4 Meanwhile, spray a frying pan with low fat cooking spray, and add the mushrooms and garlic. Season and cook them for 5 minutes, stirring frequently until the mushrooms are tender.

5 To serve, arrange two triangles of polenta on each serving plate and top with the garlic mushrooms. Garnish with a little chopped parsley.

TOP TIPS If you don't own a griddle pan, just grill the polenta triangles under a hot grill for 2–3 minutes each side. It is important to keep stirring the pan as you cook the polenta to prevent lumps from forming.

You can make polenta up to two days before you need it; keep it well covered in the fridge and griddle portions of it whenever you want.

Red lentil and aubergine curry

Serves **4 V** ❄

| **POINTS** values per recipe | **11** | calories per serving | **210** |

The lentils, aubergine and coconut combine beautifully to make a lovely rich sauce. *Preparation time 25 minutes l Cooking time 30 minutes*

low fat cooking spray
1 onion, chopped
2 garlic cloves, crushed
2 tablespoons medium curry powder
½ teaspoon salt
1 aubergine, diced
175 g (6 oz) dried, split red lentils
600 ml (20 fl oz) vegetable stock
100 ml (3½ fl oz) 88% fat free coconut milk
2 tablespoons chopped fresh coriander

1 Spray a frying pan with low fat cooking spray and gently cook the onion and garlic until softened, but not browned. Stir in the curry powder and cook for 1 minute.

2 Add the salt, aubergine, lentils and stock to the pan. Bring to the boil and simmer uncovered for 30 minutes, stirring regularly to prevent the lentils sticking.

3 By this time the lentils should be tender and mushy – if not, raise the heat and boil vigorously for 5 minutes. Add the coconut milk and coriander, and mix well. Heat through and serve.

VARIATION If you want to reduce the **POINTS** value for this curry, leave out the coconut milk and stir in 2 tablespoons of tomato purée instead. You will save 1 **POINTS** value per serving.

Zero *POINTS* value vegetable curry

Serves **4 V** ❄

| *POINTS* values per recipe | 0 | calories per serving | 125 |

Preparation time 15 minutes l Cooking time 40 minutes

1 onion, chopped
2 garlic cloves, crushed
175 g (6 oz) carrots, sliced
225 g (8 oz) leeks, sliced
225 g (8 oz) courgettes, sliced
1 aubergine, diced
350 g (12 oz) cauliflower, broken into florets
100 g (3½ oz) fine green beans, halved
175 g (6 oz) button mushrooms, quartered
2 tablespoons medium curry powder
300 ml (10 fl oz) vegetable stock
400 g can of chopped tomatoes
salt and freshly ground black pepper
2 tablespoons chopped fresh coriander, to garnish

1 Place the onion, garlic, carrots, leeks, courgettes, aubergine, cauliflower, green beans and mushrooms in a large saucepan and add the curry powder. Mix well so the vegetables become coated with the curry powder.
2 Stir in the stock and tomatoes, and season to taste. Bring to the boil and then simmer uncovered for 40 minutes, stirring from time to time.
3 Serve the curry sprinkled with chopped fresh coriander.

Hearty beef and beer casserole

Serves **4** ❄

| *POINTS* values per recipe | 13 | calories per serving | 195 |

A rich and comforting stew that is excellent with steamed leeks and a baked potato for an extra 2½ *POINTS* values. *Preparation time 30 minutes l Cooking time 1 hour*

low fat cooking spray
400 g (14 oz) lean stewing steak, cubed
2 onions, chopped finely
2 tablespoons plain flour
2 carrots, sliced finely
4 celery sticks, sliced finely
2 fresh sage sprigs, chopped (optional)
200 g (7 oz) baby button mushrooms, washed
300 ml (½ pint) beef stock
150 ml (¼ pint) beer
salt and freshly ground black pepper

1 Preheat the oven to Gas Mark 2/150°C/fan oven 130°C. Heat a non stick flameproof casserole and spray with the low fat cooking spray. Season and fry the beef on a high heat, then add the onions and stir fry for a further 5 minutes. Add the flour and stir to coat the meat.
2 Add the carrots, celery, sage, if using, mushrooms and seasoning and stir fry together for a minute or two, taking care not to let the flour burn.
3 Pour over the stock and beer and stir, incorporating any 'stuck' juices into the gravy. Cover and place in the oven for 1 hour, stirring occasionally. If the stew starts to dry out, add a little stock or water.

Apple and pork braise

Serves **4**

| **POINTS** values per recipe | **19** | calories per serving | **154** |

This easy dish has a real autumnal feel to it. Serve with mashed or baked potatoes and roasted parsnips. *Preparation time 30 minutes l Cooking time 25 minutes*

low fat cooking spray

400 g (14 oz) pork leg steaks, trimmed of all fat and diced into bite size pieces

2 small onions, chopped

2 garlic cloves, crushed

4 celery stalks, chopped finely

a small bunch of fresh sage, chopped, but reserve a few small whole leaves to garnish

450 g (1 lb) cooking apples, peeled, cored and chopped

300 ml (½ pint) vegetable stock

salt and freshly ground black pepper

1 Heat a large non stick frying pan and spray with low fat cooking spray, then stir fry the pork for a few minutes until browned on all sides.

2 Add the onions and garlic and stir fry for another 5 minutes, until softened, adding a little water if necessary to prevent them from sticking.

3 Add the celery, sage, apples, stock and seasoning. Bring to the boil, then cover and simmer for 25 minutes. Serve garnished with the reserved sage leaves.

TOP TIP To braise meat, place it in a large frying pan with a little low fat cooking spray on a low temperature. Fry the meat with any 'marinade' ingredients such as garlic and onion, allowing the meat to gently combine with the flavours. Add a little water or liquid and then simmer gently to draw out the flavours.

Roast chicken with lemon and thyme

Serves **6**

| **POINTS** values per recipe | **36½** | calories per serving | **180** |

Preparation time 40 minutes l Cooking time 1¼ hours to cook

1 medium chicken, weighing approximately 1.5 kg (3 lb 5 oz)
low fat cooking spray
3 lemons, cut into chunky wedges
2 garlic cloves, crushed
a small bunch of fresh thyme, woody stems removed, chopped
300 ml (½ pint) chicken stock
salt and freshly ground black pepper

1 Preheat the oven to Gas Mark 6/200ºC/fan oven 180ºC. Place the chicken in a roasting tray and spray with low fat cooking spray. Season and squeeze the juice from the wedges of one lemon over the skin and then place the squeezed lemon shells inside the cavity.

2 Slide your fingers under the skin of the chicken and smear the crushed garlic with a little of the thyme over the breast meat.

3 Roast for about 30 minutes, basting frequently with the juices in the tray. Remove from the oven and surround the bird with the remaining lemon wedges and sprinkle with the thyme. Spray with low fat cooking spray, season and baste with any juices from the chicken, then return to the oven for another 45 minutes, until the chicken is cooked through.

4 To test if the chicken is cooked, stick a skewer or knife into the meatiest portion of one of the thighs. The juices that run out should be clear rather than bloody.

5 When cooked, remove the chicken to a carving board, cover with foil and keep warm while you make the gravy.

6 To make gravy, drain off any excess oil in the tin then place the tin on the hob. Heat until the juices boil, then add the stock.

7 Scrape up any juices stuck to the tin with a wooden spoon or spatula and boil rapidly for a few minutes until the gravy is reduced a little. Strain the gravy into a jug and serve with the carved meat, garnished with the remaining thyme and the roasted lemon wedges.

Tuna and broccoli quiche

Serves **4** ❄

| **POINTS** values per recipe | **26** | calories per serving | **395** |

Preparation time 35 minutes l Cooking time 50 minutes + 20 minutes chilling

FOR THE PASTRY
150 g (5½ oz) plain white flour, plus 2 teaspoons for rolling
15 g (½ oz) cornflour
75 g (2¾ oz) polyunsaturated margarine
a pinch of salt

FOR THE FILLING
150 g (5½ oz) broccoli florets
185 g can of tuna in brine, drained and flaked
2 eggs
300 ml (10 fl oz) skimmed milk
salt and freshly ground black pepper

1 To make the pastry, sift the flour and cornflour into a mixing bowl. Rub in the margarine, using your fingertips, until the mixture resembles fine breadcrumbs. Add a pinch of salt and enough cold water to make a soft dough.
2 Roll out the pastry on a lightly floured surface and use it to line a 20 cm (8 inch) loose bottomed fluted flan tin. Chill the pastry in the fridge for 20 minutes.
3 Preheat the oven to Gas Mark 6/200°C/fan oven 180°C. Line the pastry case with non stick baking parchment and baking beans, and bake blind for 10 minutes. Remove the paper and the beans, and return the flan tin to the oven for 5 minutes.
4 Meanwhile, cook the broccoli in boiling water for 5 minutes, and then drain it. Arrange the broccoli and the tuna in the partially baked pastry case.
5 Reduce the oven temperature to Gas Mark 4/180°C/fan oven 160°C. Whisk together the eggs and milk with a little seasoning and pour the mixture over the broccoli and tuna. Put the flan on a baking tray and return it to the oven for 45–50 minutes, until the filling has set. Serve warm or cold.

Chick pea pilau

Serves **4 V** ❄

| **POINTS** values per recipe | **22½** | calories per serving | **415** |

Preparation and cooking time 20 minutes

low fat cooking spray
1 onion, chopped finely
1 garlic clove, crushed
300 g (10½ oz) basmati rice
1 teaspoon cumin seeds
1 teaspoon ground coriander
½ teaspoon mild chilli powder
1 teaspoon paprika
225 g (8 oz) carrots, diced finely
225 g (8 oz) courgettes, diced
227 g can of chopped tomatoes
600 ml (20 fl oz) vegetable stock
410 g can of chick peas, rinsed and drained
150 g (5½ oz) baby spinach leaves, washed and drained
2 tablespoons chopped fresh coriander
salt and freshly ground black pepper

1 Spray a large saucepan with low fat cooking spray, and add the onion and garlic. Stir in the rice, cumin seeds, ground coriander, chilli powder and paprika, and cook for 2 minutes.
2 Stir in the carrots, courgettes, tomatoes and stock, and bring to the boil. Cover, reduce the heat and simmer for 10 minutes.
3 Add the chick peas, spinach, fresh coriander and seasoning, and stir well. Cover and cook for a further 2–3 minutes, until the rice is tender and the liquid has been absorbed.

VARIATION For a nuttier version, use brown rice instead of basmati. You will need to use an extra 300 ml (10 fl oz) stock and the rice will need 40 minutes cooking time before adding the chick peas, spinach and coriander. The **POINTS** values will remain the same.

Grilled chocolate peaches

Serves **4 V**

| **POINTS** values per recipe | **10** | calories per serving | **135** |

Preparation and cooking time 10 minutes

2 fresh ripe peaches, halved and stoned
50 g (1¾ oz) plain chocolate, chopped into pieces
125 g (4½ oz) 0% fat Greek style yogurt
4 teaspoons light or dark soft brown sugar

1 Preheat the grill to High. Place the peach halves in four ramekin dishes, cut side up.
2 Evenly divide the chocolate and place inside each hollow. Spoon on the yogurt to cover the peach completely. Evenly sprinkle the sugar over the surface.
3 Grill for 4–5 minutes, until the sugar has dissolved and the surface is bubbling. Serve immediately.

Ice cream cookie sandwich

Serves **8 V**

| **POINTS** values per recipe | **33½** | calories per serving | **222** |

In this typically American dessert, chewy cookies are sandwiched together with low fat ice cream – cool and delicious! *Preparation time 10 minutes l Cooking time 10 minutes*

75 g (2¾ oz) polyunsaturated margarine
75 g (2¾ oz) caster sugar
1 egg, beaten
½ teaspoon vanilla extract
110 g (4 oz) plain flour
½ teaspoon baking powder
pinch of salt
10 g (¼ oz) ground almonds
25 g (1 oz) milk chocolate chips
1 tablespoon skimmed milk

TO SERVE
8 scoops low fat vanilla ice cream

1 Preheat the oven to Gas Mark 4/180°C/fan oven 160°C. Line two baking sheets with baking paper.
2 Cream the margarine and sugar together until pale and fluffy. Gradually beat in the egg and vanilla. Sift the flour, baking powder and salt together and fold into the mixture, followed by the ground almonds, chocolate chips and milk.
3 Place 8 spoonfuls of cookie mixture on each lined tray, leaving room between them to allow for spreading as they cook. Use the back of a spoon to flatten each spoonful into a 6 cm (2½ inch) disc.
4 Bake for 10–12 minutes until light golden brown. Cool on the baking sheets for 5 minutes then transfer to a cooling rack.
5 When cold, sandwich pairs of cookies around a scoop of vanilla ice cream and serve immediately.

TOP TIP If you want to bake these cookies for the biscuit tin, they work out at 3 **POINTS** values for two.

Chocolate orange cheesecake

Serves **10 V** ❄

| **POINTS** values per recipe | **29** | calories per serving | **162** |

Cooking time 55 minutes + 2–3 hours cooling

50 g (1¾ oz) polyunsaturated margarine, chilled
75 g (2¾ oz) plain flour, sifted with a pinch of sugar, plus extra
  for kneading
low fat cooking spray

FOR THE FILLING
50 g (1¾ oz) plain chocolate with 70% cocoa solids
250 g (9 oz) very low fat soft cheese, at room temperature
50 g (1¾ oz) icing sugar plus 1 teaspoon for dusting
1 tablespoon cornflour
grated zest of 1 orange
2 eggs

1 In a mixing bowl, rub the margarine into the flour until it resembles breadcrumbs; gradually add 2 teaspoons of cold water until the mixture starts to hold together. Turn on to a floured board and knead into a ball. Put in a plastic bag and refrigerate for 30 minutes.
2 Preheat the oven to Gas Mark 4/180°C/fan oven 160°C. Remove the base from a loose bottomed 18 cm (7 inch) cake tin, spray with the low fat cooking spray and then place on a work surface.
3 Roll and push out the pastry straight on to the base until it is about 5 mm (¼ inch) thick, then reassemble the tin. Cover with foil and scatter with baking beans. Bake for 15 minutes, then remove the foil and baking beans, and put back in the oven for 5 minutes.
4 Melt the chocolate in a heatproof bowl over a small saucepan of simmering water, being careful not to let the water touch the bowl. Beat together the cheese, sugar, cornflour, zest and melted chocolate until well blended; then whisk in the eggs.
5 Pour into the tin. Bake for 35 minutes or until just set. Leave the cheesecake to cool and then turn out and serve.

Baked chocolate custard pots

Serves **4 V** ❄

| **POINTS** values per recipe | **14½** | calories per serving | **205** |

Preparation time 20 minutes l Baking time 1 hour + 2 hours chilling

2 eggs plus 1 egg yolk
300 ml (10 fl oz) skimmed milk
50 g (1¾ oz) plain chocolate with 70% cocoa solids
25 g (1 oz) cocoa powder
25 g (1 oz) caster sugar

1 Preheat the oven to Gas Mark 2/150°C/fan oven 130°C. Half fill a roasting tin with boiling water.
2 Place the eggs and egg yolk in a bowl with the milk and beat well. Strain the mixture into a clean saucepan and heat very gently – do not boil, it just needs to get warm. Remove from the heat.
3 Grate the chocolate over the egg mixture and sift in the cocoa powder. Add the sugar and whisk well.
4 Pour the chocolate mixture into four individual ramekin dishes. Place the dishes in the roasting tin. Bake in the oven for 1 hour, until the custards have set.
5 Allow to cool and then chill for 2 hours.

TOP TIP Cooking delicate dishes in a water bath, known as a bain marie, spreads the heat, so they cook slowly for a more velvety texture, and prevents them from curdling.

Baked lemon sponges with sauce

Serves **4 V** ❄ *recommended for the sponges only.*

| **POINTS** values per recipe | **16½** | calories per serving | **235** |

Preparation time 20 minutes l Cooking time 25 minutes.

2 eggs
50 g (1¾ oz) caster sugar
100 g (3½ oz) plain flour
finely grated zest of 1 lemon

FOR THE SAUCE
juice of 1 lemon
2 tablespoons cornflour
300 ml (½ pint) water
25 g (1 oz) fructose
3 tablespoons low fat plain fromage frais

1 Preheat the oven to Gas Mark 4/180°C/fan oven 160°C. Line the base of four individual ramekin dishes with non stick baking parchment.
2 Using electric beaters, whisk together the eggs and caster sugar until the mixture is light and foamy. Sift in the plain flour and fold in with the lemon zest.
3 Divide the sponge mixture between the ramekin dishes and bake for 20 minutes.
4 To make the sauce, mix the lemon juice and cornflour to form a thin paste. Heat the water and fructose in a small pan until boiling. Add the cornflour paste and cook, stirring, until you have a smooth thickened sauce. Reduce the heat and simmer for 5 minutes. Remove from the heat and whisk in the fromage frais.
5 To serve, run a round bladed knife around the edge of each cooked sponge and carefully remove from the ramekins on to a serving plate. Peel away the baking parchment lining and drizzle over a little of the sauce.

VARIATION Use orange or lime instead of the lemon if preferred. You may however need to use 2 limes as they're not as juicy as lemons.

Apricot and lime sorbet

Serves **4 V** ❄

| **POINTS** values per recipe | **1½** | calories per serving | **25** |

A refreshing dessert on a hot day! *Preparation time 30 minutes + 5 hours freezing time*

325 g (11½ oz) fresh ripe apricots, halved and stones removed
3 tablespoons sweetener
juice of ½ lime

1 Place the apricots in a medium pan with 400 ml (14 fl oz) water and the sweetener. Bring to a simmer and cook for 20–25 minutes until soft.

2 Leave to cool and then place in a food processor or blender and blend until completely smooth.

3 Add the lime juice and check for sweetness – more sweetener or lime juice may be added according to your taste.

4 Place in a plastic sealed container and chill in the freezer. After 2 hours, whisk the mixture around with a fork, to break up the ice crystals. Repeat this again after 4 hours.

5 After 5 hours the sorbet should be ready to serve – frozen but still quite soft.

TOP TIP If you forget to whisk the sorbet or it freezes too hard, just break it up and blend in the food processor to break the ice crystals down again.

Indian spiced lamb

Serves **6**

| **POINTS** values per recipe | **31** | calories per serving | **360** |

This makes a wonderful Sunday lunch for a curry-loving family and is incredibly quick to put together if you have a food processor. Serve with some steamed broccoli. *Preparation time 10 minutes l Cooking time 1½ hours*

½ leg lamb (about 900 g/2 lb), extra trimmed
2 onions, grated or minced finely
4 teaspoons grated fresh root ginger
3 garlic cloves, minced
juice of ½ lemon (about 2 tablespoons)
150 g (5½ oz) 0% fat Greek yogurt
50 g (1¾ oz) ground almonds
250 g jar Tikka flavoured spice-blend

1 Pre-heat the oven to Gas Mark 4/180°/ fan oven 160°C.
2 Mix all the ingredients together and spread all over the lamb.
3 Place the lamb on a rack and cook in the preheated oven for 1 ½ hours.
4 If the lamb appears to be getting too black, cover with some foil.
5 Rest the lamb for about 10 minutes before carving into slices. With each slice, serve some of the crisp, spicy outside. Serve 3 slices for each portion.

Roasted root cobbler

Serves **4 V** ❄

| **POINTS** values per recipe | **22½** | calories per serving | **335** |

Preparation time 25 minutes l Cooking time 50 minutes

225 g (8 oz) carrots, cut into chunks
350 g (12 oz) swede, diced
350 g (12 oz) parsnips, diced
450 g (1 lb) leeks, sliced
150 ml (5 fl oz) vegetable stock
low fat cooking spray
295 g canned low fat condensed vegetable soup

FOR THE COBBLER
150 g (5½ oz) self raising white flour plus 2 teaspoons for rolling
2 tablespoons chopped fresh parsley and chives
40 g (1½ oz) polyunsaturated margarine
4 tablespoons low fat plain yogurt
1 tablespoon skimmed milk
a pinch of salt and freshly ground black pepper

1 Preheat the oven to Gas Mark 5/190°C/fan oven 170°C. Mix together the veg and arrange them in a non stick roasting tin. Pour in the stock and spray the vegetables with low fat cooking spray. Roast in the oven for 25 minutes.
2 Mix the canned soup with the vegetables and spoon the mixture into an ovenproof dish.
3 For the cobbler, sift the flour and stir in the herbs and seasoning. Rub in the margarine with your fingertips until the mixture resembles fine breadcrumbs. Add the yogurt and enough cold water to make a soft dough.
4 Roll out the dough on a lightly floured surface to a thickness of 1 cm (½ inch) and stamp out rounds with an 7½ cm (3 inch) cutter. Arrange them around the edge of the dish and brush with the milk. Bake for 20–25 minutes until the topping is risen and golden.

Feed the family

Mexican beef tacos

Serves **4** ❆ *for the meat sauce*

| **POINTS** values per recipe | **25½** | calories per serving | **430** |

Preparation time 15 minutes l Cooking time 15 minutes

1 large onion, sliced
350 g (12 oz) extra lean minced beef
1 teaspoon harissa or chilli paste e.g. Bart's
½ teaspoon garlic purée
400 g (14 oz) canned, red kidney beans, rinsed
400 g (14 oz) canned, chopped tomatoes with herbs
12 taco shells
salt and freshly ground black pepper
150 ml (5 fl oz) 0% fat Greek yogurt
2 limes, quartered, to serve
fresh coriander, to serve

1 Place the onion, minced beef, harissa or chilli paste and garlic in a saucepan and dry fry for 5 minutes, stirring frequently. If the mixture becomes too dry, add a few tablespoons of water just to moisten.

2 Add the red kidney beans and the chopped tomatoes. Season well and simmer uncovered for 15 minutes.

3 Heat the grill to high and warm the tacos through for about a minute. Divide the beef mixture between the tacos. Top each one with the yogurt and sprigs of coriander. Serve with a lime wedge.

TOP TIPS Taco shells are located alongside the ethnic section in the supermarket. Mexican ingredients are readily available, and most supermarkets stock their 'own label'.

Serve lots of shredded iceberg, tomato wedges and spring onions with these tacos, so that there is plenty to nibble on over this casual meal. Or bulk out the shells with a ready prepared crunchy salad.

Beef burgers

Serves **4**

| **POINTS** values per recipe | **12½** | calories per serving | **200** |

These home made burgers are easy to make and much more delicious than their shop bought counterparts. Serve on medium burger buns with lots of salad for an extra **POINTS** value of 2.

Preparation and cooking time 35 minutes

250 g (9 oz) extra lean beef mince

2 courgettes, grated

1 carrot, grated

1 large onion, grated

2 garlic cloves, crushed

1 red pepper, de-seeded and chopped

2 teaspoons English mustard

2 slices of bread, made into breadcrumbs

1 egg

low fat cooking spray

salt and freshly ground black pepper

FOR THE SPICY SALSA

½ cucumber, chopped finely

½ small red onion, chopped finely

1 red chilli, de-seeded and chopped finely

½ teaspoon caster sugar

2 tablespoons rice vinegar or white wine vinegar

1 Mix all the ingredients for the burgers together (except the low fat cooking spray) and then take tablespoons of the mixture and mould into eight burgers.

2 Spray a frying pan with the low fat cooking spray and fry the burgers in batches for about 3–4 minutes on each side or until cooked through.

3 Put them on a plate, cover with foil and keep warm while you cook the others.

4 Meanwhile, make the salsa by mixing all the ingredients together with seasoning.

5 Serve the burgers with the salsa.

Sweet and sour prawns

Serves **4**

| **POINTS** values per recipe | 8½ | calories per serving | 220 |

A delicious, low **POINTS** value version of this popular Chinese dish. *Preparation time 20 minutes l Cooking time 10 minutes*

110 g (4 oz) basmati rice
low fat cooking spray
2 garlic cloves, sliced
2 cm (¾ inch) piece of fresh root ginger, peeled and chopped
5 spring onions, chopped into long pieces
1 red pepper, de-seeded and cut into square pieces
250 g (9 oz) raw, peeled tiger prawns
200 g (7 oz) canned water chestnuts

FOR THE SAUCE
100 ml (3½ fl oz) fish stock
3 tablespoons soy sauce
1 tablespoon rice vinegar
1 tablespoon tomato purée
2 teaspoons artificial sweetener
1 teaspoon cornflour, mixed with 3 teaspoons water

1 Cook the basmati rice according to the packet instructions.
2 Heat the low fat cooking spray in a wok or large frying pan. Add the garlic, ginger, spring onions and red pepper and stir fry for 4–5 minutes.
3 Add the prawns and water chestnuts and cook for 1 minute.
4 Mix together all the sauce ingredients and pour into the wok. Stir fry for 3–4 minutes until the sauce starts to thicken.
5 Serve with the basmati rice.

TOP TIP Water chestnuts are a, sweet, crunchy bulb about the size of a walnut and sold in supermarkets and Chinese grocers.

Italian pasta salad

Serves **4 V**

| **POINTS** values per recipe | 17½ | calories per serving | 315 |

The home made pesto in this recipe is every bit as tasty as the shop bought version, but it is much lower in **POINTS** values. *Preparation and cooking time 20 minutes + chilling*

225 g (8 oz) pasta twists
75 g (2¾ oz) stoned black olives
25 g (1 oz) pine nut kernels
15 g (½ oz) fresh basil leaves
1 tablespoon olive oil
1 garlic clove, crushed
2 tablespoons fresh lemon juice
225 g (8 oz) cherry tomatoes, halved
salt and freshly ground black pepper

1 Cook the pasta according to the packet instructions. This should take about 10 minutes. Drain well.
2 To make the pesto, place the olives, pine kernels, basil leaves, olive oil, garlic, lemon juice and seasoning in a food processor. Blend until all the ingredients are chopped evenly and you have a coarse paste. If you don't have a food processor, you can use a pestle and mortar.
3 Toss the pesto into the cooked pasta along with the cherry tomatoes. Cover and chill until required.

TIP Toss the pesto with the pasta while it is still warm. The pasta will absorb the flavours better.

Turkey chow mein

Serves **4**

| **POINTS** values per recipe | 20 | calories per serving | 255 |

A twist on the take away favourite – perfect for a Friday night. *Preparation and cooking time 25 minutes*

2 teaspoons soy sauce
juice of 1 lime
125 g (4½ oz) turkey breast meat, cut into thin strips
225 g (8 oz) dried medium egg noodles
low fat cooking spray
3 garlic cloves, chopped finely
50 g (1¾ oz) mange tout, shredded
50 g (1¾ oz) ham, shredded
3 teaspoons soy sauce
6 spring onions, sliced
salt and freshly ground black pepper

1 Mix together the soy sauce, lime juice and seasoning in a small bowl. Add the turkey strips and leave to marinate for 10 minutes.
2 Cook the noodles in a large pan of boiling water for 3–5 minutes. Drain and then refresh under cold water. Drain again and reserve.
3 Heat a wok over a high heat with low fat cooking spray. Add the turkey strips and stir fry for about 2 minutes then transfer them to a plate. Wipe the wok clean.
4 Reheat the wok with low fat cooking spray, add the garlic and stir fry for 10 seconds before adding the mange tout and ham. Stir fry for 1 minute.
5 Add the noodles, soy sauce and spring onions and stir fry for 2 minutes.
6 Return the turkey to the wok and stir fry for another 3–4 minutes until the turkey is cooked. Serve immediately.

Linguine with ham and peas

Serves **4**

| **POINTS** values per recipe | 17½ | calories per serving | 325 |

A tasty and simple dish for all the family.
Preparation and cooking time 25 minutes

225 g (8 oz) linguine
2 teaspoons olive oil
100 g (3½ oz) wafer thin smoked ham, shredded
125 g (4½ oz) frozen peas
100 g (3½ oz) stoned black olives
450 g (1 lb) plum tomatoes, peeled, de-seeded and chopped finely
zest of ½ orange
2 tablespoons chopped fresh flat leaf parsley
salt and freshly ground black pepper

1 Cook the pasta in a large saucepan of boiling water for 8–10 minutes or according to the packet instructions. Drain thoroughly and mix with the olive oil.
2 Place the pasta in a large saucepan and add the ham, peas, black olives, chopped tomatoes, orange zest, parsley and seasoning. Heat through while mixing everything together.
3 Divide the pasta mixture between four warmed plates and serve immediately.

TOP TIP If you are in a hurry, use a can of chopped tomatoes instead of skinning and de-seeding fresh ones.

VARIATION Use spaghetti or tagliatelle instead of linguine for this recipe if you prefer.

Beef, mushroom and potato moussaka

(8½ POINTS VALUE)

Serves **4**

| **POINTS** values per recipe | **34** | calories per serving | **485** |

It's worth parboiling the potatoes in this recipe since it drastically reduces the cooking time.

Preparation time 25 minutes l Cooking time 35 minutes

low fat cooking spray
500 g (1 lb 2 oz) extra lean minced beef
2 garlic cloves, crushed
200 g (7 oz) mushrooms, chopped
400 g can chopped tomatoes
1 tablespoon tomato purée
600 g (1 lb 5 oz) potatoes, par-boiled for 5 minutes and sliced thinly
2 eggs, beaten
150 g tub of 0% fat Total yogurt (Greek yogurt)
100 g (3½ oz) half fat Cheddar cheese
salt and freshly ground black pepper

1 Preheat the oven to Gas Mark 4/180°C/fan oven 160°C.

2 Using a non stick pan and low fat cooking spray, brown the beef, garlic and mushrooms.

3 Add the tomatoes and tomato purée and simmer for 5 minutes. Season to taste.

4 Put half of this mixture in an ovenproof dish and cover with half of the precooked potatoes.

5 Repeat with the remaining meat and potatoes.

6 Beat the eggs, yogurt and cheese together and use this to top the moussaka.

7 Bake uncovered in the preheated oven for 35 minutes.

VARIATION You can jazz this recipe up so that it is suitable for a supper party by substituting wild mushrooms for the mushrooms in the recipe.

Chicken lasagne

Serves **4** ❄

| **POINTS** values per recipe | **26** | calories per serving | **415** |

Preparation time 45 minutes l Cooking time 25 minutes

2 teaspoons olive oil

350 g (12 oz) skinless chicken breasts, cut into bite size chunks

450 g (1 lb) leeks, sliced thinly

1 garlic clove, crushed

400 g can of chopped tomatoes

2 tablespoons tomato purée

1 teaspoon dried basil

150 ml (5 fl oz) boiling water

8 sheets no pre cook lasagne sheets

300 ml (10 fl oz) skimmed milk

25 g (1 oz) cornflour

200 g (7 oz) low fat soft cheese

25 g (1 oz) Parmesan cheese, grated

salt and freshly ground black pepper

1 Heat the oil in a non stick frying pan and add the chicken, leeks and garlic. Stir fry for 5 minutes until the chicken begins to brown.

2 Add the chopped tomatoes, tomato purée, basil, seasoning and the boiling water. Simmer for 15 minutes.

3 Preheat the oven to Gas Mark 5/190°C/fan oven 170°C.

4 Spoon half the chicken and leek mixture into a deep, ovenproof rectangular dish, and then arrange four sheets of lasagne on top. Spoon on the remaining chicken mixture and finish with the last four lasagne sheets.

5 Heat the milk until it is boiling. In a bowl, mix the cornflour to a thin paste with a little cold water. Pour the boiling milk into the bowl and then return this mixture to a clean pan and cook, whisking, until it thickens. Stir in the low fat soft cheese and then pour this cheese sauce over the top of the lasagne sheets.

6 Sprinkle the surface with the Parmesan cheese and bake in the oven for 25 minutes.

TOP TIP Lasagne is always a good standby meal to have at hand. It freezes well, so wrap up any leftovers in individual portions and pop them in the freezer for another day.

VARIATION You can use 350 g (12 oz) turkey mince for the filling instead of chopped chicken, if you prefer – it will make this dish a little less expensive. The **POINTS** values per serving will be 7.

Sweet pumpkin and peanut curry

Serves **4 V**

| **POINTS** values per recipe | 12½ | calories per serving | 209 |

Serve this hearty curry with 4 tablespoons of cooked basmati rice for an extra **POINTS** value of 3 per serving. *Preparation time 30 minutes l Cooking time 20 minutes to cook*

2 teaspoons vegetable oil

4 garlic cloves, crushed

4 shallots, chopped finely

2 teaspoons red or green Thai curry paste

600 ml (1 pint) vegetable stock

2 lime leaves, torn

2.5 cm (1 inch) piece of fresh root ginger, peeled and chopped finely

450 g (1 lb) pumpkin, peeled, de-seeded and cubed

200 g (7 oz) sweet potatoes, peeled and cubed

100 g (3½ oz) mushrooms, sliced

100 ml (3½ fl oz) low fat coconut milk

50 g (1¾ oz) roasted peanuts, chopped

3 tablespoons soy sauce

a small bunch of fresh coriander, chopped

1 Heat the oil in a large non stick pan and then fry the garlic and shallots for 10 minutes, until softened and golden, adding a little water if necessary to prevent them from sticking. Add the curry paste and stir fry for 30 seconds. Then add the stock, lime leaves, ginger, pumpkin and sweet potatoes. Bring to the boil, and then simmer for 20 minutes or until the potatoes are cooked.

2 Add the mushrooms and simmer for 5 minutes more before removing from the heat and stirring in the coconut milk, peanuts, soy sauce and coriander. Serve.

TOP TIP To prepare the pumpkin, cut it into wedges and then remove the flesh in large sections with a sharp knife. Alternatively, cut the pumpkin into strips and remove the rind with a potato peeler before cutting into chunks.

Eggy bread and tomato sandwich

Serves **1**

| **POINTS** values per recipe | **4½** | calories per serving | **305** |

Preparation and cooking time 15 minutes

1 egg
4 tablespoons skimmed milk
2 thin slices white bread
1 teaspoon olive oil
1 tomato, sliced
5 basil leaves
salt and freshly ground black pepper

1 Beat together the egg, milk and seasoning and pour into a shallow bowl. Soak the bread slices in the mixture for 5 minutes until they absorb all the liquid.
2 Heat the oil in a large non stick frying pan and add the soaked bread. Cook over a medium heat for 2–3 minutes each side, until the slices are crisp and golden.
3 Arrange the tomato slices on one slice of the cooked bread. Scatter the basil leaves over the tomatoes and lightly press the other slice of bread on top. Transfer the sandwich to a serving plate and slice in half.

Cajun potato wedges

Serves **2 V**

| **POINTS** values per recipe | **7½** | calories per serving | **260** |

Great as a starter or side dish, these crispy spicy wedges are perfectly complemented by the cooling soured cream dip and a zero **POINTS** value salsa. *Preparation time 15 minutes l Cooking time 20 minutes.*

2 x 200 g (7 oz) baking potatoes
1 teaspoon Cajun seasoning
low fat cooking spray
salt and freshly ground black pepper

FOR THE SOURED CREAM DIP
150 g (5½ oz) 0% fat Greek yogurt
2 tablespoons sour cream
1 small garlic clove, crushed
1 tablespoon chopped fresh chives

FOR THE SALSA
10 cherry tomatoes, quartered
½ red pepper, diced finely
½ green chilli, deseeded and chopped finely
1 shallot, chopped finely
1 teaspoon lemon juice

1 Preheat the oven to Gas Mark 5/190°C/fan oven 170°C.
2 Cut each potato into 8 wedges then boil in water for 5 minutes. Drain and toss with the Cajun seasoning until evenly coated. Arrange on a baking tray and spray with low fat cooking spray. Bake for 20 minutes (turning half way through) until crisp and golden brown.
3 Mix the salsa ingredients together and set aside for 10 minutes to allow the flavours to develop.
4 Blend together the yogurt, sour cream, garlic, chives and seasoning and serve as a dip for the Cajun wedges.

Spring vegetable stew

Serves **4 V**

| **POINTS** values per recipe | **9½** | calories per serving | **190** |

A fresh tasting spring stew full of cheerful colours and goodness which is simplicity itself to make. *Preparation time 2 minutes l Cooking time 20 minutes*

400 g (14 oz) new potatoes
600 ml (1 pint) boiling vegetable stock
40 g (1½ oz) pesto sauce from a jar
1 bunch spring onions, chopped roughly
2 garlic cloves, sliced into slivers
200 g (7 oz) sugar snap peas
200 g (7 oz) runner beans, cut diagonally
200 g (7 oz) baby carrots, halved or quartered lengthways
100 g (3½ oz) frozen petit pois
100 g (3½ oz) frozen, shelled broad beans
1 bunch fresh basil or mint, chopped

1 Put the potatoes in a saucepan, pour the boiling stock over and boil for 15–20 minutes until just tender.
2 Add the pesto sauce and the rest of the vegetables. Cook for 5 minutes more then serve sprinkled with the basil or mint.

TOP TIPS Pesto sauce is available in jars from the pasta sauce section of supermarkets or it can be bought from the chilled sauces or delicatessan. Pesto is also good on baked potatoes instead of butter or cheese; spread it sparingly over fish and then grill, or swirl into soup instead of fresh herbs.

VARIATIONS Use red pepper purée, hot harissa paste (1 tablespoon is 1 **POINTS** value) or tapenade instead of the pesto.

Fish and chip pie

Serves **4**

| **POINTS** values per recipe | **14** | calories per serving | **230** |

This lovely fish pie has a light golden topping of chipped potatoes – delicious! This is one for all the family to enjoy. *Preparation time 25 minutes l Cooking time 30 minutes*

370 g (13 oz) cod fillets, skinned
25 g (1 oz) sauce flour
300 ml (½ pint) skimmed milk
100 g (3½ oz) peas, cooked
salt and freshly ground black pepper

FOR THE TOPPING
400 g (14 oz) potato, par-boiled for 5 minutes, cut into
    matchstick shapes
2 teaspoons lemon juice
2 teaspoons oil

1 Preheat the oven to Gas Mark 6/ 200°C/fan oven 180°C.
2 Poach or steam the fish for 8–10 minutes, until cooked.
3 Meanwhile, put the sauce flour and milk in a saucepan and bring to the boil, whilst stirring. When a sauce is formed, simmer very gently for 5 minutes.
4 Mix together the potato, lemon juice and oil for the topping.
5 To assemble the pie, mix together the flaked fish, peas and sauce. Season well. Place in the bottom of a shallow ovenproof dish. Top with the potatoes, season again and bake, uncovered, in the preheated oven, for 30 minutes, until the 'chips' are light brown and crisp.

TOP TIP Sauce flour is now available in all major supermarkets.

Meringue fruit nests

Chocolate pudding

Serves **6 V**

| **POINTS** values per recipe | 18 | calories per serving | 155 |

The meringues are dried out – rather than baked – in a very low heat oven, so be patient! Fill them with fresh fruits for a delicious treat. *Preparation time 25 minutes l Cooking time 2–3 hours*

3 egg whites
175 g (6 oz) golden caster sugar
1 medium mango, peeled and sliced
175 g (6 oz) strawberries, sliced
1 kiwi fruit, peeled and sliced
6 tablespoons low fat aerosol cream

1 Preheat the oven to Gas Mark 1/140°C/fan oven 120°C. Line two baking sheets with non stick baking parchment.
2 Whisk the egg whites in a grease free bowl until stiff, gradually whisking in the sugar until the mixture is very glossy and stiff peaks form.
3 Fit a large piping bag with a star nozzle and fill it with the meringue mixture. Pipe three circles on each baking sheet, with a diameter of approximately 9 cm (3½ inches) to form the base of the nests. Pipe another layer around the rim of each circle to form the sides of the nests.
4 Transfer to the oven and bake for 10 minutes, and then reduce the oven temperature to Gas Mark ½/120°C/fan oven 100°C. Leave them in the oven for 2–3 hours to dry out.
5 Remove the meringues from the oven and let them cool down completely before lifting them off the parchment.
6 Mix together the prepared fruit, and use to fill the meringue nests. Finish off each one with a tablespoon of aerosol cream.

TOP TIP Unfilled meringues will keep for several weeks in an airtight tin.

Serves: **4 V** *if using vegetarian crème fraîche*

| **POINTS** values per recipe | 24½ | calories per serving | 355 |

Preparation time 10 minutes + 30 minutes standing l Cooking time 40 minutes

1 teaspoon polyunsaturated margarine
6 thin slices of white bread, crusts removed
300 ml (½ pint) skimmed milk
170 g can of evaporated milk
65 g (2¼ oz) light muscovado sugar
2 tablespoons cocoa powder
1 teaspoon vanilla extract
2 large eggs, beaten

TO SERVE
1 teaspoon cocoa powder, for dusting
4 tablespoons half fat crème fraîche

1 Grease a 1 litre (1¾-pint) baking dish with the margarine. Cut the bread into triangles and layer them in the dish.
2 In a medium saucepan, warm the milk, evaporated milk, sugar, cocoa powder and vanilla extract together, stirring to mix. Do not let the mixture get too hot – you just need to dissolve the sugar and blend in the cocoa powder. Pour in the eggs and whisk the mixture together. Pour this mixture over the bread in the baking dish. Cover and soak for about 30 minutes.
3 Preheat the oven to Gas Mark 4/ 180°C/fan oven 160°C.
4 Remove the covering from the dish and bake the pudding for 35–40 minutes, until set. Cool for a few minutes, then dust with cocoa and serve with crème fraîche.

Jam roly poly

Serves **6 V**

| **POINTS** values per recipe | **31½** | calories per serving | **270** |

This recipe will take you back to your childhood ... it's a proper stodgy, steamed version but made with polyunsaturated margarine rather than suet. The result is well worth the wait! *Preparation time 25 minutes l Cooking time 1½ hours*

low fat cooking spray
200 g (7 oz) self raising flour
½ teaspoon salt
100 g (3½ oz) polyunsaturated margarine
6 tablespoons reduced-sugar strawberry or raspberry jam

1 Half fill a steamer with water and put on to boil. Spray a piece of foil measuring 23 x 33 cm (9 x 13 inches) with the low fat cooking spray.
2 In a large bowl, mix the flour, salt and margarine together then add about 7 tablespoons of water and mix to form a light, elastic dough. Knead this very lightly until smooth. Roll out on a floured surface to an oblong 23 x 25 cm (9 x 11 inches).
3 Spread the pastry with the jam leaving a 5 mm (¼ inch) clear border all round. Brush the edges with a little skimmed milk and roll the pastry up evenly starting from one of the short sides.
4 Place the roll on the foil and wrap the foil loosely around, to allow for expansion, but seal the edges very well. Place the roll in a steamer (see Top Tip) and cover. Steam over rapidly boiling water for 1½ hours.
5 When it is cooked, remove from the foil and serve.

TOP TIP If you do not have a steamer, you can use a large pan with a close fitting lid. You could also cover the pan with foil or baking paper and then put on the lid so that it is sealed even better. Be sure to keep an eye on the water level and top it up with boiling water if necessary.

Raspberry tart

Serves **6 V**

| **POINTS** values per recipe | **13** | calories per serving | **118** |

A light but sophisticated tart that makes a perfect summer dessert for a family lunch or dinner with friends. *Preparation time 40 minutes + 20 minutes chilling*

FOR THE PASTRY
50 g (1¾ oz) polyunsaturated margarine, chilled
75 g (2¾ oz) plain flour
a pinch of sugar

FOR THE FILLING
200 g (7 oz) fresh raspberries
4 teaspoons reduced sugar, high fruit content raspberry jam

1 Make the pastry by rubbing the margarine into the flour and sugar in a mixing bowl, until the mixture resembles fresh breadcrumbs; then add 1–2 tablespoons of cold water and bring together quickly with your hand into a ball. Wrap in clingfilm and chill for 20 minutes.
2 Preheat the oven to Gas Mark 6/200°C/fan oven 180°C. Roll out the pastry straight on to, and slightly bigger than, the base of a 19 cm (7½ inch) loose bottomed flan or cake tin. Place the base back into the ring, so that the pastry edge comes slightly up the sides. Push into the corners with your fingers and up at the edge. Line with foil or baking paper and fill with baking beans.
3 Bake blind for 10 minutes. Then remove the beans and lining and bake for a further 10 minutes or until evenly golden brown.
4 Allow the pastry to cool, then arrange the raspberries on top.
5 Heat the jam in a small saucepan with 4–5 teaspoons of water and brush over the raspberries to glaze.

Plum cobbler

Serves **6 V**

| **POINTS** values per recipe | **27½** | calories per serving | **257** |

A cobbler is a rustic scone like topping that is used to top a hot fruity dessert, and makes a pleasant change from crumble. Serve with low fat custard or low fat vanilla ice cream, adding the extra **POINTS** values. *Preparation time 15 minutes l Cooking time 25 minutes*

60 g (2 oz) demerara sugar
900 g (2 lb) plums, halved and stoned
½ teaspoon ground cinnamon

FOR THE COBBLER TOPPING
125 ml (4 fl oz) skimmed milk
1 tablespoon lemon juice
175 g (6 oz) plain flour
1 teaspoon baking powder
salt
30 g (1¼ oz) caster sugar
30 g (1¼ oz) polyunsaturated margarine

1 Preheat the oven to Gas Mark 5/190°C/fan oven 170°C.
2 Mix the lemon juice into the skimmed milk and leave to stand for 5 minutes, during which time the milk will curdle – this is normal.
3 Reserve 1 tablespoon of demerara sugar for the topping, then place the remaining sugar in a pan with the plums, cinnamon and 125 ml (4 fl oz) water. Cover and simmer for 5 minutes then tip into a baking dish.
4 Sift the flour, baking powder and a pinch of salt in to a mixing bowl. Stir in the caster sugar then rub in the margarine until the mixture looks like breadcrumbs. Using a round bladed knife, add the 'soured milk' to bind the cobbler mixture to a soft and slightly sticky dough.

5 Dollop rough spoonfuls of the cobbler dough on top of the plums, then scatter with the reserved demerara sugar.
6 Place on a baking tray and bake on the centre shelf of the oven for 25 minutes until the cobbler topping is golden brown and crusty. Leave to stand for 5 minutes before serving.

VARIATION To make a rhubarb cobbler, use 750 g (1 lb 10 oz) chopped rhubarb in place of the plums, increase the sugar to 75 g (2¾ oz) and flavour with ground ginger instead of cinnamon. This will be 4 **POINTS** values per serving.

Vanilla rice pudding

Serves **4 V**

| **POINTS** values per recipe | **11½** | calories per serving | **189** |

This creamy rice pudding is delicious served hot on its own. Soya milk, now sold widely, is made from yellow soya beans. It has quite a strong flavour and adds a creaminess to recipes such as this. You can use skimmed milk if you prefer, but you will lose some of the creaminess and taste. *Preparation and cooking time 20–25 minutes*

700 ml (1¼ pints) soya milk
1 vanilla pod, split and scraped
low fat cooking spray
150 g (5½ oz) risotto rice
1½ tablespoons artificial sweetener

1 Place the milk and vanilla pod into a small saucepan and place over a medium heat.
2 Spray a medium pan with low fat cooking spray and stir in the rice. Cook over a medium heat whilst stirring, for 2–3 minutes.
3 Pour a ladle of the milk into the rice and, with the heat slightly higher so the milk bubbles constantly, stir until all the milk is absorbed. Sprinkle in a little of the sweetener with every addition of milk.
4 Keep repeating this process until all the milk is absorbed and you are left with a creamy vanilla rice pudding.

Sticky toffee fruits

Serves **2 V**

| **POINTS** values per recipe | **5½** | calories per serving | **170** |

This is a good way to use up over ripe fruit. You can use your favourite fruits in this recipe; pears, plums and pineapple are particularly good, especially with the thick and creamy fat free Greek style yogurt. *Preparation and cooking time 15 minutes*

15 g (½ oz) butter
juice of 1 orange
1 apple, cored and sliced thickly
1 small banana, sliced thickly
a pinch of ground cinnamon
1 tablespoon soft light brown sugar

1 Melt the butter in a frying pan, add the orange juice and apple. Cook for 1 minute, then add the banana and cinnamon. Cook for a further 2 minutes until soft. Remove with a slotted spoon to two serving plates.
2 Increase the heat and add the sugar. Stir until dissolved, and allow the sauce to boil rapidly to reduce and become syrupy. Spoon over the warm fruits. Serve.

Lime meringue tart

Serves **6 V**

| **POINTS** values per recipe | **27½** | calories per serving | **275** |

This classic tart is traditionally made with lemons, but this lime version gives this old favourite a new lease of life! *Preparation and cooking time 1 hour + 20 minutes chilling*

FOR THE PASTRY
125 g (4½ oz) plain white flour, plus 2 teaspoons for rolling
25 g (1 oz) cornflour
a pinch of salt
75 g (2¾ oz) polyunsaturated margarine

FOR THE FILLING
3 tablespoons cornflour
finely grated zest and juice of 3 limes
15 g (½ oz) granulated artificial sweetener
2 egg yolks

FOR THE MERINGUE
2 egg whites
50 g (1¾ oz) caster sugar

1 To make the pastry, sift the flour and cornflour along with the salt into a mixing bowl. Rub in the margarine with your fingertips until the mixture resembles fine breadcrumbs. Add enough cold water to mix to a soft dough.

2 Roll out the pastry on a lightly floured surface and use it to line a 20 cm (8 inch) loose bottomed fluted flan tin. Chill the pastry in the fridge for 20 minutes.

3 Preheat the oven to Gas Mark 6/200°C/fan oven 180°C. Line the pastry case with non stick baking parchment and baking beans and bake blind for 10 minutes. Remove the beans and lining paper and return it to the oven for 10 minutes, until the pastry is pale golden and crisp.

4 Meanwhile, to make the filling, whisk together the cornflour, 150 ml (5 fl oz) of water, lime zest and lime juice, artificial sweetener and egg yolks. Heat the mixture gently in a small saucepan over a low heat, stirring continuously, until you have a thick sauce.

5 Spoon the filling into the cooked pastry case and level it with the back of a spoon.

6 To make the meringue, place the egg whites in a clean mixing bowl and whisk them with electric beaters until stiff. Add the sugar a spoonful at a time and continue whisking until you have a thick, glossy meringue mixture.

7 Spoon the meringue over the lime filling, using the back of a spoon to swirl it over the top. Return the tart to the oven for 5–8 minutes, until the meringue is golden brown and crisp on top.

TOP TIP When baking a pastry case, line it with non stick baking parchment and baking beans. Otherwise the pastry shrinks as it cooks. If you don't have baking beans use dried pulses, such as kidney beans or marrowfat peas.

Comforting classics

Roast beef with all the trimmings

Serves **4**

| **POINTS** values per recipe | **37½** | calories per serving | **530** |

Sunday wouldn't be complete without a roast, and this recipe means you can enjoy it without using too many **POINTS** values. *Preparation and cooking time 1 hour*

600 g (1 lb 5 oz) piece of beef silverside

FOR THE ROAST VEGETABLES
450 g (1 lb) potatoes, peeled and diced
350 g (12 oz) carrots, cut into large chunks
225 g (8 oz) small parsnips, cut into quarters
1 tablespoon sunflower oil
1 teaspoon chilli flakes

FOR THE YORKSHIRE PUDDINGS
100 g (3½ oz) plain white flour
a pinch of salt
1 egg
300 ml (10 fl oz) skimmed milk
low fat cooking spray

FOR THE GRAVY
425 ml (15 fl oz) beef stock
1 teaspoon horseradish sauce
2 tablespoons cornflour

1 Preheat the oven to Gas Mark 5/190°C/fan oven 170°C. Rinse the beef and place it in a non stick roasting tin. Season well and roast for 1 hour.

2 Meanwhile, in a large mixing bowl, mix together the vegetables with the oil, a little seasoning and the chilli flakes. After 20 minutes of roasting time remove the beef from the oven and arrange the vegetables around it. Return the beef and vegetables to the oven.

3 For the Yorkshire puddings, sift the flour into a mixing bowl and make a well in the centre. Add the salt, egg and milk and whisk to form a smooth batter. Spray a 12 hole, non stick Yorkshire pudding tin with low fat cooking spray and heat it in the top shelf of the oven for 5 minutes. Carefully remove it from the oven and pour in the batter. Cook on the top shelf of the oven for 20 minutes. Time the Yorkshire puddings so they are ready at the same time as the beef.

4 When the meat and vegetables are cooked, carefully transfer them to a warmed serving platter. Pour any cooking juices into a small saucepan and skim off any fat. Add the beef stock and horseradish sauce, and heat until bubbling. Mix the cornflour with a little cold water to make a thin paste and stir it into the pan. Cook, stirring, until the gravy thickens.

5 Serve 100 g (3½ oz) of roast beef per person with the Yorkshire puddings, vegetables and gravy.

Steak, mushroom and Guinness pie

Serves **4** ❄

| **POINTS** values per recipe | **30½** | calories per serving | **330** |

A nostalgic and delicious pie. *Preparation time 35 minutes l Cooking time 2½ hours*

low fat cooking spray
2 medium onions, diced finely
1 medium carrot, sliced finely
2 celery sticks, sliced finely
2 sprigs fresh sage, chopped
200 g (7 oz) button mushrooms
4 tablespoons plain flour
400 g (14 oz) lean stewing steak, cubed
150 ml (5 fl oz) stock
150 ml (5 fl oz) Guinness
salt and freshly ground black pepper

FOR THE PASTRY
100 g (3½ oz) shop bought ready rolled puff pastry

1 Preheat the oven to Gas Mark 2/150°C/fan oven 130°C/300°F. Heat a non stick frying pan with the low fat cooking spray and fry the onions, carrot, celery and sage until softened, then remove from the heat and put into an ovenproof casserole dish.

2 In the same pan fry the mushrooms until softened and add them to the casserole dish.

3 Sprinkle the flour on a plate, season then roll the meat in it until completely covered. Spray the pan with low fat cooking spray again and fry the meat until browned all over. Add to the casserole dish. Pour the stock and Guinness over and put in the oven, covered, for 2 hours, stirring occasionally.

4 Meanwhile, place a 20 cm (8 inch) pie dish upside down on the rolled out pastry and cut out a circle slightly larger than the dish.

5 When the meat mixture is cooked, carefully transfer to the pie dish and increase the oven temperature to Gas Mark 7/220°C/fan oven 200°C.

6 Place the pastry on top of the dish, using any trimmings to make leaves for the top. Push down the pastry on to the edge of the dish to seal and 'knock up' the sides. Brush with a little skimmed milk and make a slit in the middle for the steam to escape.

7 Bake for 15–20 minutes or until risen and golden.

Chilli con carne

Serves **4** ❄

| **POINTS** values per recipe | **19½** | calories per serving | **305** |

Preparation time 25 minutes l Cooking time 1 hour to cook

350 g (12 oz) extra lean beef mince
1 tablespoon mild chilli powder
1 teaspoon ground coriander
1 onion, chopped
2 garlic cloves, crushed
175 g (6 oz) carrots, diced finely
100 g (3½ oz) button mushrooms, quartered
100 ml (3½ fl oz) red wine
400 g can of chopped tomatoes
2 tablespoons tomato purée
300 ml (10 fl oz) beef stock
410 g can of red kidney beans, drained and rinsed
salt and freshly ground black pepper
2 tablespoons chopped fresh parsley, to garnish

1 Heat a large non stick saucepan and add the mince. Dry fry for 2–3 minutes until the mince is browned. Add the chilli powder, ground coriander, onion, garlic, carrots and mushrooms, and stir well. Cook, stirring, for 5 minutes.

2 Pour in the wine, chopped tomatoes, tomato purée and stock, season, stir well and bring to the boil. Reduce the heat and simmer, stirring from time to time, for 1 hour.

3 About 5 minutes before the end of the cooking time, stir in the kidney beans. Allow them to heat through.

4 Ladle the chilli con carne into warmed bowls. Sprinkle with chopped fresh parsley and serve.

TOP TIP Make this as hot as you want, but take care! Add a little chilli powder first and then taste before adding more, it's worth remembering that the heat of the chilli develops as it cooks.

VEGETARIAN OPTION To make a vegetarian version of this chilli con carne, use vegetarian mince and a vegetable stock cube. You'll only need to cook the chilli for 30 minutes. The **POINTS** values will be 4 per serving.

Lancashire hotpot

Serves **4** ❄

| **POINTS** values per recipe | **32½** | calories per serving | **480** |

A traditional stew of lamb cutlets with thyme and a crisp and golden potato topping. *Preparation time 15 minutes l Cooking time 2½ hours*

low fat cooking spray
800 g (1 lb 11oz) potatoes, peeled and sliced thinly
600 g (1 lb 5 oz) lamb cutlets, fat removed and bones cleaned
3 medium onions, chopped finely
2 medium carrots, sliced
4 sprigs fresh thyme, chopped
1 bay leaf
a pinch of sugar
300 ml (½ pint) stock
25 g (1 oz) polyunsaturated margarine, melted
salt and freshly ground black pepper

1 Preheat the oven to Gas Mark 3/160°C/fan oven 140°C. Spray a casserole or oven proof dish with the low fat cooking spray then put a layer of potatoes in the bottom. Lay the cutlets on top.
2 Sprinkle in the onions, carrots and herbs and season well then sprinkle with sugar. Finish with the rest of the potatoes arranged over the top so that the slices overlap one another.
3 Pour in the stock and brush the top with the melted margarine. Cover and bake for 2½ hours, removing the cover for the last 40 minutes so that the potatoes crisp up and brown.

Baked lemon spring chicken

Serves **4**

| **POINTS** values per recipe | **14** | calories per serving | **226** |

A fresh tasting, quick chicken dish. Serve with courgettes and steamed, al dente baby carrots.

Preparation time 15 minutes l Cooking time 40 minutes

4 x 165 g (5¾ oz) boneless, skinless chicken breast fillets
4 spring onions, chopped finely
2 garlic cloves, crushed
2 small red chillies, de-seeded and chopped finely (optional)
grated zest and juice of 2 lemons
4 teaspoons olive oil
salt and freshly ground black pepper

1 Preheat the oven to Gas Mark 4/180°C/fan oven 160°C. Put the chicken fillets in a large baking dish lined with foil. Scatter over the remaining ingredients and fold the foil up to enclose the chicken.

2 Bake for 40 minutes. Unwrap the foil for the last 10 minutes to allow the chicken to brown.

TOP TIPS To keep meat and poultry moist, wrap it in foil, leaving a section open, and place in a baking tray. Scatter over any marinade ingredients you are using. Wrap up the chicken until it is contained in the foil then cook in the oven as required, opening the foil just before the end of cooking to allow the meat to brown. This method seals in the flavour and moisture and does not require any fat for cooking. The same method can be used for fish.

Club sandwich

Serves **2**

| **POINTS** values per recipe | **9½** | calories per serving | **405** |

Preparation and cooking time 15 minutes

2 rashers lean back bacon
1 tablespoon low fat mayonnaise
½ teaspoon Dijon mustard
3 medium slices white bread
25 g (1 oz) wafer thin turkey
4 Little Gem lettuce leaves, shredded
1 tomato, sliced
15 g (½ oz) dolcelatte cheese, crumbled
salt and freshly ground black pepper

1 Grill the bacon and drain it on kitchen paper. Combine the mayonnaise and mustard and spread this on the bread.
2 Arrange half the turkey on one slice of the bread, top with 2 lettuce leaves, a bacon rasher and half the tomato slices.
3 Place the second slice of bread on top and then top with the rest of the turkey, bacon, lettuce and tomatoes, cheese and seasoning.
4 Cover with the last slice of bread, cut into quarters and secure each with a cocktail stick.

Pizza Giardiniera

Serves **2 V**

| **POINTS** values per recipe | **9½** | calories per serving | **320** |

This is a 'fresh from the garden' pizza topped with plenty of green vegetables and oozing melted cheese. *Preparation time 20 minutes l Cooking time 12-15 minutes*

low fat cooking spray
1 bunch spring onions, sliced lengthways
110 g (4 oz) asparagus tips
60 g (2 oz) green beans, halved
60 g (2 oz) peas, defrosted if frozen
2 small courgettes, cut in ribbons (see Top tip)
23 cm (9 inch) thin and crispy pizza base
4 tablespoons tomato purée
6 tablespoons half fat grated Cheddar cheese
1 tablespoon parsley, chopped to garnish

1 Preheat the oven to Gas Mark 7/ 220°C/fan oven 200°C or according to the pizza base packet instructions.
2 Spray a frying pan with low fat cooking spray and heat until sizzling. Add the spring onions and cook stirring for 3–4 minutes until wilted. Remove from the heat.
3 Bring a large pan of water to the boil, add the asparagus and beans and cook for 3 minutes. Add the peas and courgettes and cook for a further 2 minutes. Drain thoroughly.
4 Place the pizza base on a baking sheet sprayed with low fat cooking spray and spread with the tomato purée. Top with the spring onions, vegetables and finally the cheese. Bake for 12–15 minutes until golden and bubbling.
5 Divide in two and serve garnished with parsley.

TOP TIP Use a vegetable peeler to cut ribbons along the length of the courgettes.

Persian chicken tagine

Serves **4**

| **POINTS** values per recipe | **33** | calories per serving | **575** |

A warm cinnamon and cumin flavoured casserole. Serve with 4 tablespoons of cooked rice for an extra 3 **POINTS** values per serving. *Preparation time 25 minutes l Cooking time 50 minutes*

low fat cooking spray
8 medium skinless chicken thighs
1 large onion, chopped
4 garlic cloves, crushed
1 stick celery, chopped finely
2 medium carrots, chopped finely
1 tablespoon plain flour
½ teaspoon ground cinnamon
1 teaspoon ground cumin
1 teaspoon ground turmeric
150 ml (5 fl oz) white wine
600 ml (1 pint) chicken stock
2 x 400 g cans chick peas, rinsed and drained
a bunch of fresh coriander, chopped
salt and freshly ground black pepper

1 Heat a casserole or large, heavy based saucepan on the hob and spray with the low fat cooking spray. Add the chicken thighs, season and brown on all sides, then remove and set aside. Add the onion, garlic, celery and carrots to the pan and cook for 10 minutes, until softened, stirring occasionally.
2 Mix the flour with the spices and stir in, cooking for 2 minutes. Return the chicken pieces to the pan, pour the wine and stock over, season, cover and cook on a low heat for 45 minutes.
3 Add the chick peas and cook a further 5 minutes, then sprinkle the coriander over and serve.

Toad in the hole

Serves **4**

| **POINTS** values per recipe | **24** | calories per serving | **375** |

The vegetables in this popular dish add a burst of colour. They also make it a more filling meal without adding any **POINTS** values! *Preparation time 20 minutes l Cooking time 45 minutes*

1 tablespoon sunflower oil
450 g (1 lb) low fat pork sausages
225 g (8 oz) carrots, cut into thick chunks
1 red onion, cut into wedges
4 celery sticks, cut into 5 cm (2 inch) pieces

FOR THE BATTER
100 g (3½ oz) plain white flour
a pinch of salt
1 egg
300 ml (10 fl oz) skimmed milk
1 teaspoon dried mixed herbs

1 Preheat the oven to Gas Mark 6/200°C/fan oven 180°C. Place the oil in a 23 cm (9 inch) square non stick baking tin. Arrange the sausages, carrots, onion and celery in the base of the tin. Roast in the oven for 20 minutes.
2 Meanwhile, make the batter. Sift the flour and salt into a mixing bowl, and make a well in the centre. Add the egg, milk and herbs and whisk to form a smooth batter.
3 Remove the sausages and vegetables from the oven and pour over the batter. Return the tin to the oven for 20–25 minutes, until the batter is well risen and deep golden.
4 Cut the toad in the hole into quarters and serve hot.

VARIATION Try using other zero **POINTS** value vegetables for this dish, such as open cup mushrooms or chunks of leeks or courgettes.

Chicken korma

6½ POINTS VALUE

Serves **4** ❄ *for up to 1 month*

| *POINTS* values per recipe | **26** | calories per serving | **420** |

A favourite for those who like their curries creamy and not too hot! *Preparation time 12 minutes l Cooking time 15–20 minutes*

low fat cooking spray
1 onion, chopped
2 garlic cloves, crushed
½ teaspoon chilli powder
½ teaspoon turmeric
½ teaspoon ground coriander
1 teaspoon ground cumin
1 green cardamom pod, crushed
a pinch of salt

500 g (1 lb 2 oz) skinless, boneless chicken breasts, cut into bitesize pieces
1 teaspoon tomato purée
1 teaspoon peeled and grated fresh root ginger
½ teaspoon garam masala
400 ml (14 fl oz) chicken stock
250 g (9 oz) basmati rice
100 ml (3½ fl oz) reduced fat coconut milk
25 g (1 oz) flaked almonds
salt and freshly ground black pepper

1 Heat a medium pan and spray with low fat cooking spray. Add the onion and garlic and cook for 2–3 minutes.

2 Add the spices, salt and chicken and stir well to completely coat the chicken.

3 Add the tomato purée, ginger, garam masala and chicken stock and bring to the boil. Simmer gently for 15 minutes. Cook the rice according to the packet instructions.

4 Add the coconut milk and flaked almonds and continue to simmer for another 5 minutes. Check the seasoning and serve with the cooked basmati rice.

VARIATION For Prawn Korma, omit the chicken and use 400 g (14 oz) of prawns instead. The *POINTS* values per serving will be 6.

Fish stew with saffron

Serves **6**

| **POINTS** values per recipe | **8½** | calories per serving | **125** |

A wholesome, tasty fish dish. Serve with a medium crusty brown roll to soak up the juices – but don't forget to add 2 extra **POINTS** values!
Preparation time 15 minutes l Cooking time 12 minutes

low fat cooking spray
3 shallots, chopped
1 leek, sliced
2 carrots, diced
2 celery sticks, diced
400 g (14 oz) canned chopped tomatoes
a pinch of saffron threads
600 ml (1 pint) hot fish stock
400 g (14 oz) cod, cut into bite size pieces
200 g (7 oz) raw prawns
salt and freshly ground black pepper
a bunch of fresh parsley, chopped

1 Spray a medium pan with low fat cooking spray and add the shallots, leek, carrots and celery. Stir fry for 3–4 minutes until starting to soften.

2 Add the chopped tomatoes and cook for another 2–3 minutes.

3 Meanwhile, add the saffron threads to the hot fish stock and leave to infuse for 2 minutes.

4 Pour the saffron infused stock into the pan and add the cod and prawns.

5 Season and bring to a simmer. Simmer for 4–5 minutes until the prawns turn pink and the cod turns white.

6 Check the seasoning, stir in the chopped parsley and serve.

Spaghetti vongole

Serves **4**

| **POINTS** values per recipe | **10½** | calories per serving | **305** |

Vongole is Italian for clams, which are small shellfish available fresh from your fishmonger or ready shelled in brine in most supermarkets. The wine and stock make a great flavoured sauce that clings to the pasta. *Preparation and cooking time 20 minutes*

175 g (6 oz) spaghetti
1 x 142 g jar clams in brine
50 ml (2 fl oz) dry white wine
100 ml (3½ fl oz) fish or vegetable stock
2 tablespoons parsley, chopped
2 teaspoons crushed, dried chillies
salt and freshly ground black pepper

1 Bring a large pan of salted water to the boil, add the spaghetti and cook for 10 minutes or 2 minutes less than the packet instructions. Drain and rinse with plenty of boiling water.
2 Put the clams in a large pan with the white wine and stock and cook for 2 minutes until hot.
3 Add the spaghetti to the pan with the parsley, chillis and salt and pepper and cook, stirring over a medium heat for 2 minutes more. Divide between four bowls and serve immediately.

TOP TIP By slightly undercooking the pasta initially it will absorb some of the wine and clam juices when you return it to the pan, giving extra flavour to the pasta.

VARIATIONS If you can get fresh clams use 450 g (1 lb). To prepare, scrub the clams and discard any that have damaged shells or don't shut when tapped as they are dead. To cook, place them in a large pan with the white wine and stock, bring to the boil and cook for 3 minutes until just opened. Shake the pan occasionally to assist the heat distribution. Add 2 tablespoons of chopped tarragon instead of the parsley for a light aniseed flavour.

Sweet onion tart

Serves **4 V**

| **POINTS** values per recipe | **15½** | calories per serving | **305** |

Serve with 200 g (7 oz) new potatoes and a crisp green salad, adding on 2 **POINTS** values per serving. *Preparation time 15 minutes + 30 minutes cooling l Cooking time 1 hour 10 minutes*

FOR THE PASTRY
50 g (1¾ oz) polyunsaturated margarine
50 g (1¾ oz) plain flour
50 g (1¾ oz) wholemeal flour
a pinch of salt

FOR THE SWEET ONION FILLING
low fat cooking spray
1 kg (2 lb 4 oz) onions, sliced very thinly
a small bunch of thyme, chopped
2 medium eggs
150 ml (5 fl oz) skimmed milk
2 teaspoons French mustard
salt and freshly ground black pepper

1 Make the pastry by rubbing the margarine into the flours and salt until the mixture resembles fresh breadcrumbs then add about 1 tablespoon of water and mix the dough quickly into a ball with your hand. Wrap in clingfilm and chill in the refrigerator for 30 minutes.

2 Meanwhile, heat a large frying pan and spray with the low fat cooking spray then add the onions, thyme and seasoning and stir fry for 2 minutes over a high heat.

3 Cover the pan with a piece of baking paper tucked down the sides to seal the onion mixture in, then cover with a lid and sweat over the lowest possible heat for 20 minutes. Pull the paper to one side occasionally and stir to make sure the mixture is not sticking to the pan, adding a little water to prevent this if necessary.

4 Preheat the oven to Gas Mark 5/190°C//fan oven 170°C. Roll the pastry out to a circle about 5 mm (½ inch) thick and use to line a 19 cm (7½ inch) loose bottomed flan tin. Line with foil then fill with baking beans.

5 Bake for 15 minutes then remove the beans and foil lining and bake for a further 10 minutes or until evenly golden brown.

6 Meanwhile, beat the eggs with the milk, mustard and seasoning in a jug.

7 Spoon the cooked onions into the pastry case, pour the egg mixture over and bake for 20 minutes until the filling is set and lightly golden.

VARIATION Try filling the tart with roasted zero **POINTS** value vegetables instead of the onions. The **POINTS** values will remain the same.

Aubergine cannelloni

Serves **4 V** ❄ *after step 4*

| **POINTS** values per recipe | **14½** | calories per serving | **259** |

There is no pasta in this 'cannelloni' recipe: slices of grilled aubergine are used to lower the **POINTS** values. *Preparation time 35 minutes l Cooking time 35 minutes*

100 g (3½ oz) long grain rice
2 large aubergines
low fat cooking spray
250 g (9 oz) low fat cottage cheese with onion and chives
a small bunch of fresh parsley, chopped
400 g (14 oz) canned chopped tomatoes with herbs
1 onion, chopped finely
2 garlic cloves, chopped finely
a small bunch of fresh basil, leaves removed and larger ones torn
100 g (3½ oz) half fat Cheddar cheese, grated
salt and freshly ground black pepper

1 Put the rice on to cook as instructed on the packet.

2 Meanwhile, preheat the grill to high and slice the aubergines into thin slices lengthways. Season and spray with low fat cooking spray. Grill for 5 minutes on one side, then turn and grill for 2 minutes more, until golden.

3 Preheat the oven to Gas Mark 4/180°C/fan oven 160°C. Drain the rice and mix in a large bowl with the cottage cheese, parsley, seasoning and half the tomatoes.

4 Spray a non stick frying pan with the low fat cooking spray and fry the onion and garlic for 5 minutes. Add a little water if necessary to prevent them from sticking. Add the rest of the tomatoes and bring to the boil. Simmer for 5 minutes, then season and add the basil.

5 Place 2–3 tablespoons of the cottage cheese mixture on each aubergine strip and roll up into a cylinder. Place in one layer in a lasagne dish and pour over the tomato and basil sauce. Scatter with the Cheddar cheese.

6 Bake for 35 minutes, until the Cheddar cheese is golden and bubbling. Allow to stand for a few minutes before serving.

Apple and blackberry tarts

Serves **6**

| **POINTS** values per recipe | **18** | calories per serving | **190** |

Make these wonderful fruit-filled tarts with filo pastry, brushed with a delicately flavoured olive oil, rather than butter. *Preparation and cooking time 25 minutes*

6 fresh filo pastry sheets
4 tablespoons light or delicately flavoured olive oil
350 g (12 oz) baking apples, peeled, cored and sliced
1 tablespoon lemon juice
125 g (4½ oz) blackberries
powdered sweetener, to taste

TO SERVE
4 tablespoons 0% fat Greek yogurt
2 teaspoons icing sugar
mint or blackberry leaves (optional)

1 Preheat the oven to Gas Mark 5/190°C/fan oven 170°C.
2 Unfold the filo pastry sheets and cut the pastry into six piles, measuring approximately 10 cm (4 inches) square. Layer these filo squares in six individual tartlet tins, brushing each pastry sheet with a little olive oil. Pack a little crumpled foil in each tartlet tin, and bake for 8–10 minutes until the pastry is golden brown.
3 Meanwhile, cook the apples in a saucepan with the lemon juice and a couple of tablespoons of water until tender – about 5–6 minutes. Remove from the heat and stir in the blackberries. Cool slightly and then sweeten to taste with the powdered sweetener.
4 Remove the foil from the filo pastry tarts and spoon in the apple and blackberry filling. Top each one with a tablespoon of Greek yogurt or serve it on the side. Sprinkle with icing sugar and serve, decorated with mint or blackberry leaves, if desired.

VARIATION Fill the tarts with soft summer fruits – a mixture of 175 g (6 oz) strawberries, 175 g (6 oz) raspberries and 125 g (4½ oz) blueberries would taste lovely. The **POINTS** values per tart remain the same.

Tiramisu

Serves **8 V** ❄

| **POINTS** values per recipe | **16½** | calories per serving | **125** |

Perhaps this dessert has been somewhat over done but that's only because it is so delicious. Here is a low **POINTS** value version. *Preparation time 20 minutes + minimum 1 hour chilling*

18 sponge fingers
300 ml (½ pint) strong black coffee
200 g (7 oz) virtually fat free fromage frais
150 g (5½ oz) Quark cheese
50 g (1¾ oz) icing sugar
1 teaspoon vanilla essence
25 g (1 oz) cocoa powder
25 g (1 oz) dark chocolate, grated finely

1 Line the base and sides of a 450 g (1 lb) loaf tin with clingfilm. Place a layer of sponge fingers in the bottom and pour a third of the coffee over.
2 Put the rest of the fingers in a separate bowl and pour over the rest of the coffee. Beat half the fromage frais with the Quark, icing sugar and vanilla until smooth. Spread half of this mixture over the sponge fingers in the tin.
3 Sprinkle with a little cocoa powder then top with a layer of the soaked sponge fingers. Spread the remaining half of the cheese mixture over and sprinkle again with cocoa powder.
4 Top with the remaining sponge fingers, cover with clingfilm and chill for at least 1 hour. Turn out on to a serving plate and remove the clingfilm. Spread with the remaining fromage frais and sprinkle with the grated chocolate.

Mango and berry pavlova

Serves **4–6 V**

| **POINTS** values per recipe | **11** | calories per serving | **139** |

Preparation time 15 minutes l Baking time 1 hour

3 egg whites
4½ tablespoons artificial sweetener
450 g (1 lb) low fat raspberry yogurt
150 g (5½ oz) raspberries
125 g (4½ oz) blueberries
2 mangoes, stoned, peeled and sliced

1 Preheat the oven to Gas Mark 3/160°C/fan oven 140°C.
2 Place the egg whites in a completely clean, grease free bowl and whisk until stiff.
3 Gradually whisk in the sweetener, one tablespoon at a time, until you have a stiff meringue mixture.
4 Spoon the mixture onto a greaseproof lined baking sheet in a circle, with a slight dip in the centre.
5 Reduce the oven temperature to Gas Mark 1/140°C/fan oven 120°C and bake for 1 hour.
6 Turn off the oven and leave the pavlova inside until the oven has cooled (baking pavlova just before you go to bed is a good idea, then it can be left in the oven overnight).
7 When you are ready to serve the pavlova, gently remove the greaseproof paper and place on a serving plate.
8 Spoon over the yogurt and top with the fruits. Serve immediately.

Honey 'ice cream'

Serves **4 V** ❄

| **POINTS** values per recipe | **16½** | calories per serving | **210** |

This is not really an ice cream as it has no cream in it, but it is so creamy and delicious that no other name fully describes it. *Preparation time 10 minutes + cooling + minimum 4 hours freezing*

300 ml (½ pint) low fat custard made with 2 tablespoons reduced-sugar custard powder and 300 ml (½ pint) skimmed milk
100 g (3½ oz) clear honey
410 g can 'Light' evaporated milk, chilled

1 Make up the custard according to the pack instructions but using the honey as the sweetener instead of sugar. Leave to cool.
2 Whisk the evaporated milk until thick and doubled in volume then fold into the cool custard mixture with a metal spoon.
3 Turn into a freezer proof container and freeze until firm around the edges. Whisk with a fork to break up the ice crystals, then freeze again until firm.

TOP TIP If you have an ice cream maker then put the mixture into it to freeze; there is no need to whisk to break up the crystals as the machine will do it for you.

VARIATIONS For a raspberry, strawberry, or mixed summer berry ice, purée 225 g (8 oz) of your chosen berries, fresh, frozen or canned and then fold into the custard. For a ripple effect, only partially fold the berries in at the end to give a swirled pattern. The **POINTS** values per serving will be 5.

Baked Alaska

Serves **4 V**

| **POINTS** values per recipe | **12** | calories per serving | **150** |

A very impressive and delicious dessert for a dinner party. It looks fantastic and is one of the easiest puddings to make. *Preparation time 10 minutes l Cooking time 8–10 minutes*

1 medium (75 g/2¾ oz) sponge flan case
400 ml (14 fl oz) low fat vanilla ice cream
3 egg whites
3 tablespoons sugar

1 Preheat the oven to Gas Mark 8/230°C/fan oven 210°C.
2 Place the sponge flan case on a baking tray.
3 In a clean bowl, whisk the egg whites until stiff then gradually add the sugar and keep whisking until you have a stiff, glossy mixture.
4 Quickly spoon the ice cream into the flan case and press into a rounded shape.
5 Cover the whole flan case and ice cream with meringue and make a pattern of little peaks by patting the meringue with the back of a spoon.
6 Place in the oven and cook for 8–10 minutes until golden. Keep a close eye on this as it will change from golden to black very quickly!
7 Serve immediately.

TOP TIP When whisking egg whites, the bowl must always be completely grease free or the whites will not stiffen.

Make it special

Trout stuffed with couscous

Serves **4**

| **POINTS** values per recipe | 28½ | calories per serving | 450 |

A very impressive Moroccan inspired dish, where the couscous and spices are cooked inside the fish. Serve with a fresh, light zero **POINTS** value salad. *Preparation time 25 minutes l Cooking time 15–20 minutes*

low fat cooking spray
1 small onion, chopped finely
2 garlic cloves, crushed
1 teaspoon ground cumin
100 g (3½ oz) couscous
300 ml (½ pint) vegetable stock
1 tablespoon chopped fresh parsley
2 tablespoons chopped fresh mint
4 trout, 200 g (7 oz) each, gutted, heads removed and boned
40 g (1½ oz) flaked almonds, chopped
salt and freshly ground black pepper

1 Preheat the oven to Gas Mark 6/200°C/fan oven 180°C.
2 Heat a frying pan and spray with low fat cooking spray. Fry the onion for 2–3 minutes, until softened.
3 Add the garlic and cumin and cook for 1 minute more.
4 Add the couscous, vegetable stock and herbs and stir well. Bring to the boil then remove from the heat and leave for 10–15 minutes, to allow the couscous to absorb the stock.
5 Season the trout and fill each one with the couscous.
6 Place the fish in a shallow baking dish that has been sprayed with low fat cooking spray. Sprinkle with the chopped almonds.
7 Bake in the oven for 15–20 minutes until the fish is tender.

Salmon and asparagus nibbles

Makes **20**

| **POINTS** values per recipe | 19½ | calories per serving | 125 |

These are really tasty canapes to serve at parties and with a **POINTS** value of just 1 each you can afford to indulge! *Preparation and cooking time 10 minutes*

1 x 100 g pack asparagus spears, trimmed and halved
1 x 10 pack mini white pitta breads, sliced in halves
4 tablespoons tomato purée
250 g (9 oz) low fat cream cheese
zest of 1 lime, grated finely
75 g (2¾ oz) smoked salmon, cut in thin strips
4 spring onions, chopped finely
salt and freshly ground black pepper
1 lime, cut into wedges to garnish

1 Preheat the grill to medium. Bring a large pan of cold water to the boil, add the asparagus spears and cook for 3 minutes until just tender. Drain and rinse with cold water.
2 Toast the pitta breads under the grill for 2 minutes, turning once until warm. Spread each with a little tomato purée.
3 Mix the cream cheese with the lemon zest and salt and freshly ground black pepper. Spoon a teaspoon of this mixture onto each pitta half, then top with the smoked salmon and asparagus spears and garnish with spring onions. Serve with lime wedges to squeeze over.

TOP TIP Get everything ready before you toast the pitta breads so that you can serve them still warm.

Duck breasts with pepper sauce

Serves **4**

| **POINTS** values per recipe | **16** | calories per serving | **171** |

This wonderfully rich, creamy sauce goes well with succulent duck breasts – for a special occasion. Serve accompanied by zero **POINTS** value vegetables of your choice. *Preparation and cooking time 25 minutes*

low fat cooking spray
4 medium, skinless duck breasts (approx 125 g/4½ oz each), fat removed
1 red onion, diced
2 tablespoons green peppercorns
100 ml (3½ fl oz) chicken stock
4 tablespoons low fat fromage frais

1 Spray a frying pan with the low fat cooking spray and heat. Cook the duck breasts for 5–6 minutes on each side, depending on how rare you like your meat. Remove from the pan and keep warm.
2 Add the onion to the pan and cook for 2–3 minutes before adding the remaining ingredients.
3 Simmer for 3–4 minutes.
4 Slice the duck breasts and serve with the sauce poured over.

TOP TIP To cook duck breast, score the flesh and cook in a pan over a high heat. Cook it until it is slightly pink for a really tender, flavoursome meat. Remember to drain off any fat before serving.

Prawn cocktail

Serves **4**

| **POINTS** values per recipe | **8** | calories per serving | **120** |

Year in, year out, prawn cocktail ranks as one of our all time favourite starters – probably because it tastes so good! *Preparation time 10 minutes*

6 tablespoons plain low fat yogurt
2 tablespoons tomato ketchup
1 tablespoon tartare sauce
350 g (12 oz) cooked, peeled prawns, defrosted if frozen
1 bag of herb salad
1–2 teaspoons seasoned rice vinegar dressing or white wine vinegar
salt and freshly ground black pepper

TO GARNISH
1 tablespoon chopped fresh parsley (optional)
1 lime or lemon, sliced into wedges

1 In a medium bowl, mix together the yogurt, tomato ketchup and tartare sauce. Add the prawns and stir gently to coat. Season.
2 Toss the salad leaves in the seasoned vinegar dressing or white wine vinegar, and then arrange on serving plates. Alternatively, shred the leaves and divide them between four attractive glasses.
3 Top the salad leaves with the prawn mixture. Garnish with chopped parsley, if using, and lime or lemon wedges, and serve.

VARIATION For a spicier version, stir ½ teaspoon of de-seeded, finely chopped fresh green chilli and a tablespoon of chopped fresh coriander into the prawn mixture, omitting the parsley. The **POINTS** values will remain the same.

Red pepper and basil cheesecake

Serves **6 V** ❄

| **POINTS** values per recipe | 21 | calories per serving | 225 |

Not all cheesecakes have to be sweet, try this savoury version and you'll be hooked! *Preparation time 35 minutes l Cooking time 20 minutes + 10 minutes cooling*

FOR THE PASTRY
100 g (3½ oz) plain white flour plus 2 teaspoons for rolling
1 tablespoon cornflour
50 g (1¾ oz) polyunsaturated margarine
a pinch of salt

FOR THE FILLING
3 red peppers, de-seeded and halved
350 g (12 oz) low fat plain cottage cheese
2 eggs
2 tablespoons torn fresh basil
salt and freshly ground black pepper

1 To make the pastry, mix the flour and cornflour together in a bowl. Rub in the margarine with your fingertips, until the mixture resembles fine breadcrumbs. Add the salt and then stir in enough cold water to make a soft dough.

2 Preheat the oven to Gas Mark 5/190°C/fan oven 170°C. On a lightly floured surface, roll out the pastry so it is big enough to line the base and sides of a 20 cm (8 inch) fluted loose bottomed flan tin.

3 Lift the pastry into the tin and prick the base with a fork. Line with non stick baking parchment and baking beans. Bake blind for 10 minutes. Remove the paper and the beans, and return the pastry to the oven for 10 minutes.

4 Meanwhile, grill the peppers under a high heat, skin side up, until the skins blacken and blister. Transfer the peppers to a polythene bag and seal. When they are cool enough to handle, peel off the skins and roughly chop the flesh.

5 Place the peppers, cottage cheese, eggs, basil and seasoning in a food processor and blend until smooth. Remove the pastry flan case from the oven and spoon in the pepper filling.

6 Return the flan to the oven for 20 minutes, until the filling has set and is firm to the touch. Allow to cool for 10 minutes before slicing into wedges to serve.

TOP TIP If you don't have a food processor, chop the red pepper very finely and push the cottage cheese through a sieve. Mix them together with the eggs, seasoning and basil as in step 5 before spooning into the flan case.

Malaysian BBQ pork

Serves **6**

| **POINTS** values per recipe | **25½** | calories per serving | **225** |

Serve with very lightly steamed pak choi or spinach. *Preparation time 25 minutes + a minimum of 2 hours marinating l Cooking time 45 minutes*

900 g (2 lb) lean pork fillet, trimmed of all fat
2 spring onions, chopped, to garnish

FOR THE MARINADE
1 tablespoon clear honey
150 ml (5 fl oz) dark soy sauce
50 ml (2 fl oz) medium dry sherry
150 ml (5 fl oz) stock
1 tablespoon soft brown sugar
1 cm (½ inch) piece of fresh root ginger, peeled and sliced finely
1 small onion, chopped

1 Mix all the marinade ingredients together in a pan. Bring to the boil then simmer for 15 minutes. Let cool.

2 Put the pork fillets in a shallow dish that is large enough to hold them side by side. Pour the marinade over. Cover and chill in the refrigerator for at least 2 hours, preferably overnight, turning the meat several times.

3 Preheat the oven to Gas Mark 6/200°C/fan oven 180°C. Drain the pork, reserving the marinade. Place the meat with the marinated onion and ginger bits on top of it on a rack over a roasting tin and pour water into the tin to a depth of 1 cm (½ inch).

4 Place the tin in the oven and roast for 20 minutes. Remove the meat from the oven and brush with the marinade again then put back and roast for another 20 minutes or until cooked through.

5 Meanwhile, put the marinade liquid into a saucepan, bring to the boil then simmer for 5 minutes. Serve the pork in slices either hot or cold with the marinade as a sauce and garnished with chopped spring onions.

Moroccan spiced rice with lamb

Serves **4**

| **POINTS** values per recipe | 26½ | calories per serving | 430 |

With the authentic combination of ginger, cinnamon and mint, this Moroccan dish is absolutely delicious. *Preparation time 30 minutes l Cooking time 20 minutes*

350 g (12 oz) lean lamb mince

1 onion, sliced

2 garlic cloves, crushed

½ teaspoon ground ginger

½ teaspoon ground cinnamon

1 teaspoon paprika

1 aubergine, diced

225 g (8 oz) courgettes, diced

225 g (8 oz) long grain white rice

400 ml (14 fl oz) lamb stock

450 g (1 lb) plum tomatoes, skinned, deseeded and diced

2 tablespoons chopped fresh mint, plus a few extra leaves, to garnish

1 Heat a heavy based non stick frying pan and add the lamb mince. Dry fry for 5 minutes, draining off any excess fat. Add the onion, garlic, ginger, cinnamon and paprika, and stir well.

2 Add the aubergine, courgettes, rice and stock, and bring to the boil. Cover and simmer for 20 minutes until the stock has been absorbed and the rice is tender.

3 Add the tomatoes and mint, and heat through. Spoon the mixture into a warmed serving dish and scatter with a few extra mint leaves.

TOP TIP The easiest way to skin tomatoes is to plunge them into boiling water for a few seconds – the skins will then peel off easily.

Sage and orange turkey escalopes

Serves **4** ❄

| **POINTS** values per recipe | 12½ | calories per serving | 235 |

Preparation time 15 minutes l Cooking time 30 minutes

4 x 150 g (5½ oz) turkey escalopes

low fat cooking spray

1 red onion, cut into thin wedges

300 ml (10 fl oz) fresh orange juice

1 tablespoon wholegrain mustard

½ teaspoon dried sage

150 ml (5 fl oz) chicken stock

1 orange, sliced

1 tablespoon cornflour

salt and freshly ground black pepper

1 Season the turkey escalopes on both sides.

2 Heat a large non stick frying pan and spray it with low fat cooking spray. Add the turkey to the pan and cook for 2–3 minutes on each side, until lightly browned. Add the onion wedges to the pan and cook for a further 2 minutes.

3 Add the orange juice, mustard, sage and chicken stock. Arrange the orange slices over the escalopes and bring the liquid to the boil. Reduce the heat, cover and cook for 20 minutes.

4 Mix the cornflour to a thin paste with a little cold water and stir this into the pan. Cook, stirring, until the sauce thickens a little. Transfer the escalopes to warmed plates and spoon the sauce over them to serve.

TOP TIP If you have difficulty finding turkey escalopes, try using turkey breast steaks instead, but hammer them flat with the flat end of a rolling pin. The **POINTS** values will remain the same. Use juice from freshly squeezed oranges if you can for this recipe.

Thai beef salad

Serves **8**

| **POINTS** values per recipe | **17** | calories per serving | **135** |

A warm salad with a touch of spice! This is a great lunch party dish. *Preparation time 15 minutes l Cooking time 5 minutes*

low fat cooking spray
500 g (1 lb 2 oz) lean beef fillet steak, cut into strips
2 garlic cloves, chopped finely
2 cm (¾ inch) piece of fresh root ginger, peeled and chopped finely
1 green chilli, de-seeded and chopped finely
juice of 1 lemon
1 tablespoon fish sauce (nam pla)
2 x 300 g (10½ oz) ripe mangoes, peeled and chopped
½ large cucumber, cut into strips
100 g (3½ oz) beansprouts
1 iceburg lettuce, shredded

1 Heat a wok or large frying pan and spray with low fat cooking spray. Add the steak, garlic, ginger and chilli and stir fry over a high heat for 3–4 minutes.
2 Pour in the lemon juice and fish sauce and continue to stir fry until the juices are sizzling.
3 Remove from the heat and lift out the steak with a slotted spoon. Place in a bowl with the remaining ingredients and toss together.
4 Place on a large platter and pour over the liquid from the wok.

VARIATION Try replacing the beef with the same quantity of prawns. The **POINTS** values will be 1½ per serving.

Thai prawn parcels

Makes **10**

| **POINTS** values per recipe | **10½** | calories per parcel | **60** |

These parcels are a delicious, savoury treat. They're really easy to do and only 1 **POINTS** value each! *Preparation time 20 minutes l Cooking time 15 minutes*

200 g (7 oz) prawns
2 tablespoons freshly chopped coriander
125 g (4½ oz) filo pastry
low fat cooking spray
1 tablespoon red Thai curry paste
salt and freshly ground black pepper

1 Place the prawns, coriander and seasoning in a blender or food processor and blend briefly until coarsely chopped. Preheat the oven to Gas Mark 6/200°C/fan oven 180°C.
2 Cut the pastry into squares measuring roughly 10–13 cm (4–5 inches); you need 30 squares in total. Place one square on a board and spray with low fat cooking spray. Spray two more squares and stack them on top of the first square.
3 Spread a small amount of Thai paste over the centre of the pastry and then top with about 1 tablespoon of the prawn mixture. Bring the sides of the pastry up and pinch together.
4 Spray with a little low fat cooking spray and place on a baking sheet.
5 Repeat with the remaining pastry and prawn mixture. Bake in the oven for 15 minutes until golden.

Chilli crab and mango salad

Serves **4**

| **POINTS** values per recipe | **12½** | calories per serving | **205** |

This recipe is based on a South East Asian salad and is delicious. *Preparation time 5 minutes*

240 g (8½ oz) fresh crab meat or 2 x 120 g cans white crabmeat, drained
1 medium cucumber, grated
8 small pink radishes, halved and sliced thinly
2 medium ripe mangos or papayas, peeled and sliced
2 teaspoons caster sugar
1½ teaspoons fish or soy sauce
1 teaspoon crushed dried chilli
juice of 2 limes
1 small red chilli, de-seeded and chopped
50 g (1¾ oz) roasted peanuts, chopped
a small bunch of chives or coriander, chopped
salt

1 Put all the ingredients except the chilli, peanuts and chives or coriander in a bowl and toss together gently. Pile on to serving plates, then sprinkle with the chilli, peanuts and chives or coriander and serve.

Chicken Kiev

Serves: **4**

| **POINTS** values per recipe | **18½** | calories per serving | **280** |

Serve with 100 g (3½ oz) low fat chips and zero *POINTS* value vegetables such as fine green beans, cauliflower or carrots – or all three! Add 2½ *POINTS* values per serving. *Preparation time 20 minutes l Cooking time 35–40 minutes*

low fat cooking spray

4 medium, skinless, uncooked chicken breasts, each weighing about 150 g (5½ oz)

125 g tub low fat soft cheese with garlic and herbs

2 tablespoons plain white flour

1 medium egg, beaten with 2 tablespoons cold water

50 g (1¾ oz) fresh white breadcrumbs

salt and freshly ground black pepper

1 Preheat the oven to Gas Mark 5/190°C/fan oven 170°C. Mist a baking dish or baking sheet with low fat cooking spray.

2 Put the chicken breasts, well spaced apart, between sheets of clingfilm or greaseproof paper. Use a meat mallet or rolling pin to beat them out until flattened, but avoid bashing them until they break up. Remove the clingfilm or paper.

3 Divide the soft cheese into four equal portions. Place the cheese portions on the chicken breasts, towards the wider end of the chicken. Season. Roll up the breasts, folding in the sides to encase the cheese. Use cocktail sticks to secure them.

4 Roll the chicken parcels in the flour and then dip them into the beaten egg mixture. Finally, roll them in the breadcrumbs and place in the dish or on the baking sheet.

5 Bake for 35–40 minutes, until golden brown and thoroughly cooked. To check, pierce the chicken with a skewer or sharp knife – the juices should run clear. Remove the cocktail sticks before serving.

VARIATION For an extra garlic hit, spread ½ teaspoon of garlic purée over each chicken breast before adding the cheese. The *POINTS* values will remain the same.

Chicory and blue cheese tart

Serves **4 V** ❄

| **POINTS** values per recipe | **14½** | calories per serving | **211** |

A lovely combination of flavours and textures that makes this an interesting lunch. Serve with a big mixed zero **POINTS** value salad. *Preparation time 35 minutes l Cooking 40–45 minutes*

15 g (½ oz) polyunsaturated margarine
4 heads of chicory, sliced in half lengthways
450 g (1 lb) potatoes, peeled and cut in pieces
1 teaspoon English mustard
50 g (1¾ oz) blue cheese, crumbled
1 egg
150 ml (¼ pint) skimmed milk
salt and freshly ground black pepper

1 Preheat the oven to Gas Mark 7/220°C/fan oven 200°C. Melt the margarine in a non stick frying pan and gently fry the chicory with a lid on for 20 minutes, until softened.
2 Meanwhile, boil the potatoes for about 20 minutes, until cooked. Drain and mash with the mustard and seasoning.
3 Line a 20 cm (8 inch) loose bottomed cake tin with non stick baking parchment, pile in the mash and press down to make a base. Bake in the oven for 15 minutes, until it has formed a crust.
4 Arrange the braised chicory on top of the potato base and scatter with the blue cheese. In a jug, beat together the egg and milk with some seasoning. Pour over the chicory and return to the oven for a further 10–15 minutes, until the top is golden.

Steak and chips with Béarnaise sauce

Serves **2** ❄

| **POINTS** values per recipe | **20** | calories per serving | **704** |

Preparation and cooking time 45 minutes

700 g (1 lb 9 oz) potatoes, peeled and chopped into chips
low fat cooking spray
sea salt
2 medium lean beef fillet steaks

FOR THE BÉARNAISE SAUCE
3 tablespoons white wine vinegar
1 shallot, diced
6 black peppercorns
1 teaspoon dried tarragon
2 egg yolks
1 teaspoon Dijon mustard
150 g (5½ oz) low fat soft cheese
1 tablespoon chopped fresh tarragon

1 Preheat the oven to Gas Mark 7/220°C/fan oven 200°C.
2 Boil the potatoes in a pan of water until just tender. Drain on kitchen paper. Spray a baking sheet with low fat cooking spray and then put the potatoes on it. Spray the chips again and sprinkle with sea salt. Cook in the oven for 15 minutes. Turn them all, then cook for another 10–15 minutes until they are golden.
3 Meanwhile, put the vinegar, shallot, peppercorns and dried tarragon into a small pan with 2 tablespoons of water. Bring to the boil and simmer until very little liquid is left. Strain and reserve.
4 Put the egg yolks into a bowl over a pan of simmering water. Whisk in the mustard. Gently whisk in the vinegar liquid and finally the soft cheese, a little at a time. If at any stage the sauce starts to look grainy, just pour in a little boiling water and whisk furiously – it will come back together. Stir in the fresh tarragon. Keep warm.
5 Grill the steak to your liking and serve with the chips and Béarnaise sauce.

Onion and rosemary Tarte Tatin

Serves **6 V**

| **POINTS** values per recipe | **32½** | calories per serving | **250** |

A really tasty tart – caramelised onions with a hint of rosemary, on top of luscious, light puff pastry. Serve with a crisp, zero **POINTS** value green salad. *Preparation time 20–25 minutes l Cooking time 15 minutes*

low fat cooking spray
1 large onion, halved and sliced thickly
1 large red onion, halved and sliced thickly
2 garlic cloves, sliced
leaves from 3–4 fresh rosemary sprigs
350 g (12 oz) ready made puff pastry
salt and freshly ground black pepper

1 Preheat the oven to Gas Mark 7/ 220°C/fan oven 200°C.
2 Heat the low fat cooking spray in a medium pan and add the onions and garlic. When they start to cook turn the heat down to very low and cover the pan. Cook for 15–20 minutes, stirring occasionally, until they start to caramelise. Season well.
3 Add the rosemary to the pan and stir in. Pour the onion mixture into a 23 cm (9 inch) flan tin.
4 Roll out the pastry and cut to fit the tin. Place on top of the onions and tuck in the edges.
5 Bake for 12–15 minutes until the top is golden.
6 Turn out on to a plate so the onions are on top. Serve warm.

Chocolate mocha mousse

Serves **4 V**

| **POINTS** values per recipe | **13** | calories per serving | **147** |

These rich, fluffy mousses look great in espresso cups with crème fraîche and a pinch of cocoa powder. *Preparation time 30 minutes + minimum 30 minutes chilling*

50 g (1¾ oz) plain cooking chocolate (preferably 70% cocoa solids), broken into pieces
1 tablespoon instant coffee, dissolved in 2 tablespoons boiling water, or 2 tablespoons very strong real coffee
4 teaspoons golden syrup
2 egg whites
140 g (5 oz) low fat soft cheese, at room temperature
4 teaspoons half fat crème fraîche, to serve
1 teaspoon cocoa powder, to serve

1 Place the chocolate in a large heatproof bowl, with the coffee and golden syrup. Set over a small saucepan of simmering water until the chocolate melts. Stir together and remove from the heat. Allow to cool slightly – about 10 minutes – until warm but not hot.
2 In a separate bowl, whisk the egg whites until stiff.
3 Whisk the soft cheese and melted chocolate together until smooth. Gently fold in the egg whites.
4 Spoon into four serving glasses, espresso cups or pots and refrigerate for at least 30 minutes, until chilled and set. Decorate each mousse with a teaspoon of crème fraîche and a dusting of cocoa powder to serve.

TOP TIP To whisk egg whites use two eggs that have been left at room temperature and a large mixing bowl that is clean and dry. Separate the eggs and put the whites in the bowl, making sure they are completely free of yolk. Use a whisk (either hand held or electric) and beat until the egg whites are stiff and form peaks when lifted.

Strawberry syllabub $2\frac{1}{2}$ POINTS VALUE

Serves **2** **V** ✳ *(see tip)*

| **POINTS** values per recipe | 5 | calories per serving | 80 |

In the summer months, when fresh strawberries are in abundance, make the most of them as they are both delicious and low in **POINTS** values.
Preparation and cooking time 15 minutes + 30 minutes chilling

175 g (6 oz) fresh strawberries, hulled and sliced
1 tablespoon granulated artificial sweetener
1 tablespoon port
175 ml (6 fl oz) low fat strawberry fromage frais

1 Reserve 1 strawberry and place the remaining strawberries in a food processor with the sweetener and port. Blend until smooth.
2 Place the fromage frais in a mixing bowl and stir in the strawberry purée.
3 Divide the syllabub mixture between two small dishes and chill for 30 minutes. Decorate each one with slices of the reserved strawberry before serving.

TOP TIP You can freeze this mixture to make a superb ice cream. Take it out of the freezer 20 minutes before serving.

Red cherry and ginger slice

Serves **8**

| **POINTS** values per recipe | **29½** | calories per serving | **200** |

Member Janet Smith from Scarborough in North Yorkshire has devised this indulgent dessert to keep sweet cravings at bay. It uses low fat ingredients to keep the **POINTS** values in check, though you'd never guess it was a Weight Watchers pudding. *Preparation time 25 minutes + several hours chilling*

50 g (1¾ oz) **polyunsaturated margarine**
150 g (5½ oz) **Rich Tea or Morning Coffee biscuits**
½ teaspoon **ground ginger**
4 tablespoons **boiling water**
12 g sachet of **powdered gelatine**
397 g can of **cherry pie filling**
4 teaspoons **artificial sweetener**
500 g carton **virtually fat free fromage frais**
25 g (1 oz) **crystallised ginger**

1 Line an 18 cm (7 inch) loose based cake tin with clingfilm.

2 Melt the margarine and stir in the crushed biscuits and ground ginger. Tip them into the prepared tin and press down evenly over the base. Chill in the refrigerator.

3 Put 4 tablespoons of just boiled water into a bowl and sprinkle in the gelatine. Stir to disperse, then allow 4–5 minutes for it to dissolve into a completely clear liquid.

4 Tip the cherry pie filling into a mixing bowl and add the gelatine liquid, stirring thoroughly. Add the sweetener, then fold in the fromage frais. Pour this mixture over the biscuit base and spread out evenly. Cover and chill for several hours, or overnight, to set.

5 Just before serving, carefully lift from the tin and remove the clingfilm. Cut into eight portions and decorate with finely chopped crystallised ginger.

VARIATIONS Try a different pie filling, such as blackcurrant or raspberry. Use stem ginger in syrup, well rinsed, instead of the crystallised ginger.

White chocolate dreamcake

Serves **8** ❄

| **POINTS** values per recipe | **35** | calories per serving | **205** |

A sumptuously creamy, beautiful pink mousse.
Preparation and cooking time 20 minutes + chilling time + 2 hours setting

100 g (3½ oz) reduced fat digestive biscuits
50 g (1¾ oz) polyunsaturated margarine, melted

FOR THE TOPPING
100 g (3½ oz) white chocolate, broken into pieces
400 ml (14 fl oz) low fat plain yogurt
11 g sachet powdered gelatine
300 g can raspberries in syrup

TO GARNISH (OPTIONAL)
a few fresh raspberries
fresh mint leaves

1 Pulverise the biscuits in a food processor, add the melted margarine then press into a 20 cm (8 inch) loose bottomed flan tin and chill.

2 Melt the chocolate in a bowl set over a pan of simmering water. Put the yogurt in a bowl and stir in the chocolate. Sprinkle the gelatine over 6 tablespoons of boiling water in a small pan then heat gently and stir until dissolved. Cool a little and then stir into the yogurt mixture.

3 Drain 6 tablespoons of the syrup from the raspberries and discard, then add the rest of the syrup along with the berries to the yogurt mixture. Pour into the biscuit base and chill for at least 2 hours until set.

4 Serve decorated with whole raspberries and mint leaves, if using.

Chocolate Victoria sponge

Makes **8** slices ❋ *sponges only*

| **POINTS** values per recipe | **17½** | calories per serving | **145** |

There is something very appealing about a chocolate cake, and this fat free sponge isn't as naughty as it looks! *Preparation time 25 minutes l Baking time 20 minutes*

3 eggs
75 g (2¾ oz) caster sugar
75 g (2¾ oz) plain white flour
25 g (1 oz) cocoa powder

FOR THE FILLING
3 tablespoons reduced sugar strawberry jam
100 ml (3½ fl oz) 0% fat Greek style plain yogurt

TO DECORATE
1 teaspoon icing sugar
15 g (½ oz) plain chocolate curls

1 Preheat the oven to Gas Mark 4/180°C/fan oven 160°C. Line the base of two 19 cm (7½ inch) round non stick cake tins with non stick baking parchment.
2 Place the eggs and caster sugar in a mixing bowl and whisk with electric beaters for 5 minutes, until you have a pale, fluffy mixture – when you lift the whisk, it should leave a trail.
3 Sift in the flour and cocoa powder and fold them in using a metal spoon, taking care not to knock too much air out. Divide the mixture between the two tins and bake for 20 minutes, until the sponges are firm and springy to the touch. Transfer the cakes to a wire rack to cool completely.
4 When cool, spread one of the cakes with the jam, top with the yogurt and place the second cake over the top. Put the cake on a serving plate and dust the top with icing sugar, and then scatter the chocolate curls over the top.

VARIATION Real chocolate lovers can use low fat chocolate yogurt for the filling instead of Greek yogurt. The **POINTS** values per serving will remain the same.

Time to bake

Quick and easy wholemeal bread

Makes **2** *medium loaves which cut into about 16 slices each* **V** ❄

| **POINTS** values per loaf | 20 | calories per slice | 95 |

Home made bread has many advantages over its shop bought equivalents including being less expensive and containing fewer additives. It is tasty, satisfying and, most importantly, you know exactly how many **POINTS** values are in it. This bread is delicious served with any of the scrumptious soups in this book or toasted and spread with reduced sugar jam or marmalade for an extra ½ **POINTS** value per heaped teaspoon.

Preparation time 15 minutes + 45 minutes–1 hour rising l Cooking time 35–40 minutes

900 g (2 lb) plain wholemeal flour
10 g (¼ oz) salt
15 g (½ oz) soft brown sugar
15 g (½ oz) fresh yeast or 10 g (¼ oz) dried yeast
600 ml (1 pint) warm water
low fat cooking spray

1 Mix the flour, salt and sugar together in a large bowl. Make a well in the centre.

2 Mix the yeast into a wet paste with a little warm water and pour into the well with a little more of the water.

3 Mix together with your hands, adding more water if it is too dry, until you have a slippery dough that comes away from the bowl in a smooth ball. Different flours vary in their absorbency so add the water a bit at a time in case the dough becomes too wet and sticky.

4 Divide the dough between two 13 x 23 cm (5 x 9 inch) bread tins that have been warmed and sprayed with low fat cooking spray. Cover with a clean, floured tea towel and leave in a warm place until the dough has risen by more than a half, usually around 45 minutes–1 hour.

5 Preheat the oven to Gas Mark 6/200°C/fan oven 180°C. Sprinkle the loaves with flour and bake for 35–40 minutes. Check that they are cooked by tapping the bottom – they should sound hollow.

TOP TIPS This recipe makes two medium loaves – one to eat and one to wrap in a plastic bag and freeze for up to 3 months. Uncooked bread will rise if you leave it in the fridge but it will take 24 hours, so it is not absolutely necessary to put it in a warm place but it does speed up the process. If you put it in an airing cupboard, on top of the boiler or on top of the oven, then the dough will rise quickly giving a more open texture than if left in the kitchen for, say, 1½ hours, when it rises very gently.

VARIATIONS Your bread will vary greatly depending on the flour that you use so try different brands and types or try mixing types, for example use half white and half wholemeal flour, or half white and half rye flour. Organic and stone ground flours are well worth a try as most give a lovely texture and flavour. Always use a 'strong' bread flour, as this means that it has a high gluten content which will make it rise better.

Tomato bread

Serves **6 V** ❄

| **POINTS** values per recipe | 17 | calories per serving | 189 |

This recipe contains no yeast so there's no waiting! It makes a delicious savoury bread that's ideal with soup or stews. *Preparation time 25 minutes l Cooking time 15 minutes*

225 g (8 oz) plain flour, plus extra for dusting
a pinch of salt
3 teaspoons baking powder
25 g (1 oz) sun dried tomatoes, soaked for 10 minutes in boiling water, then drained and chopped
4 spring onions, chopped finely
200 ml (7 fl oz) skimmed milk
2 tablespoons olive oil
salt and freshly ground black pepper

1 Preheat the oven to Gas Mark 7/220°C/fan oven 200°C. Sift the flour, salt and baking powder into a large bowl. Grind in a little black pepper and stir in the chopped sun dried tomatoes and spring onions.

2 Mix 150 ml (¼ pint) of the milk and the oil together and add to the flour mixture. Gently combine to make a soft and manageable dough, adding the extra milk if necessary.

3 On a lightly floured surface, roll out the dough to about 2.5 cm (1 inch) thick. Form into a round about 15 cm (6 inches) in diameter. Score into six triangles with a knife, taking care not to cut all the way through the dough.

4 Place on a baking tray, lined with non stick baking paper and bake for 12–15 minutes, until the bread is risen and golden.

Garlic and coriander naan bread

Makes **8 V** ❄

| **POINTS** values per recipe | 21 | calories per serving | 190 |

These puffy naan breads are an ideal accompaniment to a lovely saucy curry instead of rice, or they can be split open and filled as an alternative to a sandwich. *Preparation time 15 minutes + 1½ hours rising l Cooking time 5 minutes*

400 g (14 oz) plain flour, plus 1 tablespoon for kneading and 1 tablespoon for rolling
1 teaspoon fast action yeast
1 teaspoon salt
150 ml (5 fl oz) low fat natural yogurt
2 garlic cloves, crushed
3 tablespoons chopped fresh coriander

1 Mix the flour with the yeast and 1 teaspoon salt in a large bowl. Make a well in the centre and pour in the yogurt, then add up to 125 ml (4 fl oz) warm water, to bring together as a soft dough. Turn out onto a lightly floured surface and knead for 3 minutes until soft and springy. Stretch out the dough and scatter with the garlic and coriander. Knead again until evenly distributed throughout the dough.
2 Return the dough to the bowl and cover with cling film. Leave to rise in a warm place for 1½ hours or until doubled in bulk.
3 Preheat the oven to Gas Mark 8/230°C/fan oven 210°C. Place two large baking sheets in the oven to preheat.
4 Divide the dough into 8 pieces. Roll each one out on a lightly floured surface to an oval shape, measuring about 12 x 18 cm (4½ x 7 inches). Bake the naan bread on the preheated baking sheets for 5 minutes, or until puffy and browned in patches. Serve warm.

TOP TIP To freeze the naan breads, wrap them individually in clingfilm once cooled, then freeze in a plastic bag for up to one month.

Fruit scones

Serves **8 V** ❄

| **POINTS** values per recipe | **22½** | calories per serving | **185** |

For a special treat, serve each scone with a teaspoon of reduced-sugar strawberry jam and a tablespoon of low fat aerosol cream. This will add 1 **POINTS** value per serving. *Preparation and cooking time 20 minutes*

low fat cooking spray
225 g (8 oz) self raising white flour
pinch of salt
50 g (1¾ oz) polyunsaturated margarine
25 g (1 oz) golden caster sugar
50 g (1¾ oz) sultanas or raisins
1 medium egg
4 tablespoons skimmed milk

1 Preheat the oven to Gas Mark 7/220°C/fan oven 200°C. Mist a baking sheet with low fat cooking spray.

2 Sift the flour and salt into a large mixing bowl. Add the margarine and rub it in with your fingertips until the mixture resembles fine breadcrumbs. Stir in the sugar and sultanas or raisins.

3 Beat the egg and milk together and add just enough to the rubbed in mixture to give a soft, but not sticky dough. Knead lightly for a few moments, but avoid over handling it.

4 On a lightly floured surface roll out the dough so that it is about 2 cm (¾ inch) thick – it's a mistake to roll it out too thinly. Cut into eight rounds using a 5 cm (2 inch) cutter, re-rolling the dough if necessary. Place these rounds on the baking sheet and brush the tops with the remaining egg and milk mixture.

5 Bake for 10–12 minutes until risen and golden brown. Cool on a wire rack for about 10–15 minutes. These scones are at their best when served while still warm.

VARIATION Use chopped ready to eat dried apricots or dates instead of the sultanas or raisins. The **POINTS** values will remain the same.

Carrot cake with orange icing

Makes **8** slices **V** *if using vegetarian cheese* ❄

| **POINTS** values per recipe | 24 | calories per slice | 190 |

Carrot cake with its moist texture and natural sweetness, is always popular. This version has a zesty orange icing to really get the tastebuds tingling. *Preparation time 15 minutes + cooling l Cooking time 20 minutes*

low fat cooking spray
2 medium eggs
100 g (3½ oz) caster sugar
50 g (1¾ oz) polyunsaturated margarine, melted
175 g (6 oz) carrots, grated
100 g (3½ oz) self raising flour, sifted
1 teaspoon ground cinnamon
½ teaspoon ground nutmeg

FOR THE ORANGE ICING
50 g (1¾ oz) low fat soft cheese
25 g (1 oz) icing sugar
zest of 1 medium orange and 1 tablespoon of the juice

1 Preheat the oven to Gas Mark 5/190°C/fan oven 170°C. Spray an 18 cm (7 inch) round cake tin with the low fat cooking spray, line the base with baking paper then spray again.
2 Whisk the eggs and sugar together until light and fluffy. Gradually whisk in the melted margarine then add all the remaining cake ingredients.
3 Pour into the tin and bake for 20 minutes or until golden brown and firm to the touch. Turn out of the tin and leave on a wire rack to cool.
4 Make the icing by beating together the soft cheese, sugar, orange zest and juice then spread over the cooled cake.

TOP TIP Carrot cake will keep for several days in an airtight container.

Oatmeal biscuits

Makes **12** biscuits **V** ❄

| **POINTS** values per recipe | 13½ | calories per serving | 70 |

Make a batch of these delicious, crunchy biscuits and freeze them, then just remove one when you want a snack, allowing a little defrosting time. *Preparation time 10 minutes l Cooking time 15 minutes*

50 g (1¾ oz) plain white flour,
   plus 2 teaspoons for dusting
a good pinch of bicarbonate of soda
100 g (3½ oz) oatmeal
2 teaspoons light soft brown sugar (optional)
25 g (1 oz) raisins (optional)
25 g (1 oz) polyunsaturated margarine
5 tablespoons hot water

1 Heat the oven to Gas Mark 7/220°C/fan oven 200°C. Sift together the flour, bicarbonate of soda, oatmeal and sugar, if using. Stir in the raisins, if using.
2 Mix together the margarine and hot water, stirring until the margarine has melted. Beat this mixture into the dry ingredients to make a firm, but not dry dough. If necessary, add extra dribbles of hot water.
3 Turn out the dough on to a wooden board dusted with a little flour. Roll out to 5 mm (¼ inch) thickness. Cut the dough into neat squares, measuring about 5 cm (2 inches).
4 Line a heavy baking sheet with non stick baking parchment and place the oatmeal biscuits on top. Prick each one 2 or 3 times with a fork. Bake in the oven for 15 minutes until firm, and then transfer to a wire tray to cool completely.

TOP TIP You need old fashioned oatmeal for these biscuits to give them a lovely crisp texture. Most supermarkets stock it these days, or try the health food shops.

Fruit and nut bites

Makes **20** slices **V**

| **POINTS** values per recipe | 20½ | calories per slice | 60 |

Anne Wilkinson, a Member from Harrogate in North Yorkshire, is a retired Health Visitor. She developed this recipe from one originally created for her children as a healthier alternative to real sweets. *Preparation time 10 minutes + 2 hours standing time*

50 g (1¾ oz) dried mango slices
100 g (3½ oz) blanched almonds
75 g (2¾ oz) raisins
175 g (6 oz) ready to eat dried apricots
1 tablespoon cocoa powder
1 tablespoon cold tea
approximately 4 sheets of rice paper

1 In a blender or food processor, blend together the mango slices, almonds, raisins, apricots, cocoa and cold tea.
2 Divide the mixture into two, and place between sheets of rice paper, levelling the mixture out by hand, then flattening and spreading out with a rolling pin, so that the mixture is about 5 mm (¼ inch) thick.
3 Leave for about 2 hours, then cut into pieces with a sharp knife or scissors to make 20 bites.
4 Store in an airtight container.

TOP TIP Rice paper can be bought from supermarkets and good kitchenware suppliers. It is edible.

No-fat bara brith

Serves **14 V** ❄

| **POINTS** values per recipe | 39 | calories per slice | 200 |

Christine Parkman from Barry in South Glamorgan has developed a delicious low fat version of a Welsh family favourite, Bara brith, a moist dark fruit cake. Since becoming a Member, Christine has improved her health and fitness and feels much better for it! *Preparation time 10 minutes + overnight standing l Cooking time 1¼–1½ hours*

250 g (9 oz) dark muscovado sugar
250 g (9 oz) mixed dried fruit
250 ml (9 fl oz) cold tea
low fat cooking spray
300 g (10½ oz) self raising flour
1 egg, beaten

1 Put the sugar and dried fruit into a large mixing bowl and cover with the cold tea. Stir well, then cover and allow to stand overnight.
2 Next day, preheat the oven to Gas Mark 4/180°C/fan oven 160°C. Grease a 1 kg (2 lb 4 oz) loaf tin with low fat cooking spray and line with greaseproof paper.
3 Gradually add the flour and egg to the soaked fruit mixture. When thoroughly mixed, transfer to the prepared tin and bake for 1¼ hours. To test that the cake is cooked, insert a skewer into the centre of the cake – it should come out clean. If not, return to the oven for another few minutes.
4 Cool in the tin on a wire rack, and when completely cold, turn out, wrap in foil and keep for 2–3 days before cutting.

TOP TIP The cake is moist enough to eat alone but if you wish, spread it with 1 teaspoon of low fat spread adding a further ½ **POINTS** value per slice.

Italian chocolate cake

Serves **8**

| **POINTS** values per recipe | 33½ | calories per serving | 230 |

This is a fantastically chocolately cake, and the semolina adds a lovely nutty crunch. *Preparation time 15 minutes l Cooking time 35 minutes*

low fat cooking spray
110 g (4 oz) polyunsaturated margarine
110 g (4 oz) caster sugar
2 eggs, separated
25 g (1 oz) self raising flour
60 g (2 oz) cocoa, 1 teaspoon reserved for dusting
60 g (2 oz) dry semolina
4 tablespoons skimmed milk

1 Preheat the oven to Gas Mark 4/180°C/fan oven 160°C. Spray a 20 cm (8 inch) spring form cake tin with low fat cooking spray and line the base with non stick baking parchment.
2 Using an electric whisk, cream the margarine and sugar together until pale and smooth – you should notice a change in the colour. Beat the egg yolks together and gradually whisk in, beating between additions until combined.
3 Sift the flour and cocoa into the bowl, add the semolina and the milk. Use a large metal spoon to carefully fold in until combined.
4 Whisk the egg whites until they hold stiff peaks. Add a spoonful to the cake mixture and fold in to slacken it, then carefully fold in the remaining egg white.
5 Pour the mixture into the prepared tin and bake for 30–35 minutes until firm to the touch. Cool in the tin.
6 Remove the cake from the tin, dust with the reserved cocoa powder and serve in slices.

Banana cake

Serves **10 V** ❄ *cake for up to 1 month (the filling cannot be frozen)*

| **POINTS** values per recipe | 26 | calories per serving | 168 |

Preparation time 25 minutes l Baking time 30 minutes + cooling

150 g (5½ oz) low fat soft cheese
4 tablespoons artificial sweetener
3 medium eggs, separated
2 soft bananas, peeled and mashed with a fork
200 g (7 oz) polenta, cooked according to packet instructions
½ teaspoon baking powder
low fat cooking spray

FOR THE FILLING
150 g (5½ oz) low fat soft cheese
1½ teaspoons artificial sweetener
grated zest of 1 orange
1 banana
juice of ½ lemon

1 Preheat the oven to Gas Mark 4/180°C/fan oven 160°C.
2 Cream together the low fat soft cheese and the sweetener and then whisk in the egg yolks and mashed banana.
3 Fold in the polenta and baking powder. Whisk the egg whites in a separate bowl, until stiff. Fold them into the polenta mixture.
4 Spray two 18 cm (7 inch) tins with low fat cooking spray and line the base with greaseproof paper. Divide the mixture between two tins and bake for 30 minutes or until firm to the touch.
5 Allow the cakes to rest for 5 minutes and then remove from the tins. Leave to cool on a cooling rack.
6 For the filling, cream together the low fat soft cheese, sweetener and orange zest and spread over one of the cakes.
7 Slice the banana and toss in the lemon juice before placing on top of the creamy filling. Place the other cake on top and serve.

Luscious lemon fairy cakes

Makes **9** cakes **V** ❄

| **POINTS** values per recipe | 16 | calories per serving | 105 |

The fresh, zesty flavour of lemons make these little cakes a popular treat. *Preparation time 10 minutes l Baking time 15 minutes*

75 g (2¾ oz) self raising white flour
50 g (1¾ oz) polyunsaturated margarine
50 g (1¾ oz) caster sugar
1 egg, beaten
finely grated zest of 1 lemon
1 tablespoon fresh lemon juice

FOR THE TOPPING
1 tablespoon lemon curd
1 tablespoon boiling water

1 Preheat the oven to Gas Mark 5/190°C/fan oven 170°C. Line a 9 hole bun tin with paper cases.

2 Sift the flour into a bowl. In a separate mixing bowl beat the margarine and caster sugar together, until you have a pale and fluffy mixture. Add the beaten egg, lemon zest and lemon juice with 1 tablespoon of the flour and mix well.

3 Add the remaining flour to the lemon mixture and fold it in thoroughly. Divide the mixture between the paper cases and bake for 15 minutes, until the sponges are springy to the touch.

4 While the cakes are still warm, mix the lemon curd with the boiling water and brush this over the surface of the cakes. Allow them to cool before serving.

Black Forest gateau

Serves **8 V** *if using vegetarian fromage frais* ❋

| **POINTS** values per recipe | 34½ | calories per serving | 240 |

A low fat version of this classic chocolate cake.
Preparation time 20 minutes + approximately 1 hour cooling time l Cooking time 25 minutes

FOR THE CHOCOLATE CAKE
low fat cooking spray
100 g (3½ oz) polyunsaturated margarine
50 g (1¾ oz) soft brown sugar
1 teaspoon vanilla essence
25 g (1 oz) low fat drinking chocolate
2 medium eggs
100 g (3½ oz) self raising flour

FOR THE FILLING
1 tablespoon icing sugar
200 g (7 oz) virtually fat free fromage frais
425 g can stoned cherries in syrup, drained with 2 tablespoons
   syrup reserved, and cut in half
2 tablespoons kirsch (optional)
1 tablespoon cocoa powder, to dust

1 Preheat the oven to Gas Mark 4/180°C/fan oven 160°C and spray an18 cm (7 inch) cake tin with the low fat cooking spray.

2 Cream together the margarine and sugar then add the vanilla and chocolate and then the eggs, one at a time and beat well together. Sieve in the flour, fold into the mixture and spoon into the prepared tin. Bake for 25 minutes or until springy to the touch and a skewer inserted into the centre comes out clean.

3 Turn the cake out on to a cooling rack and allow to cool completely (about 1 hour) then slice in half to make 2 thinner cakes.

4 For the filling, stir the icing sugar into the fromage frais. Spoon 2 tablespoons of the juice from the cherries over one of the sponges with the kirsch, if using.

5 Thickly spread the fromage frais on the sponge and top with the drained cherries. Put the other sponge cake on top and gently press down. Dust the top with cocoa powder and serve, or chill then serve.

Rich dark fruit cake

Makes **20** slices **V** ❄

POINTS values per recipe	**61**	calories per slice	**275**

We all have a favourite rich fruit cake recipe – often handed down through the generations. But at times when we want to have that special celebration cake without the high fat content, isn't it great to have an alternative recipe which means you can stick to tradition without it sticking to the hips! *Preparation time 25 minutes l Cooking time 1¾ hours*

350 g (12 oz) ready to eat prunes
6 tablespoons brandy or sherry
finely grated zest and juice of 1 large lemon
finely grated zest and juice of 1 large orange
200 g (7 oz) dark muscovado sugar
4 medium eggs
1 tablespoon black treacle
1 medium cooking apple, peeled and grated
350 g (12 oz) plain flour
2 teaspoons baking powder
2 teaspoons mixed spice
½ teaspoon ground nutmeg
800 g (1 lb 11 oz) luxury dried mixed fruits
6 tablespoons semi-skimmed milk

1 Heat the oven to Gas Mark 4/180°C/fan oven 160°C. Line a deep 23 cm (9 inch) round cake tin with greaseproof or parchment paper.
2 Purée the prunes in a food processor or liquidiser, together with the brandy or sherry, lemon and orange zest and juice. Transfer to a bowl and whisk in the sugar and eggs until the mixture becomes light and fluffy. Whisk in the treacle.
3 Use a metal spoon to stir in the apple, flour, baking powder and spices. Finally mix in the dried fruit and enough milk to form a soft dropping consistency. Transfer to the prepared tin, levelling out the surface.

4 Bake in the centre of the oven for 45 minutes, then reduce the oven temperature to Gas Mark 3/160°C/fan oven 140°C and continue to cook for 1 hour or until the cake is well risen and a skewer inserted in the centre comes out clean.
5 Leave the cake to cool in the tin before removing and discarding the paper. Wrap the cake in fresh paper or foil and store in an airtight tin. The cake is best left for at least a day to mature before cutting.

TOP TIP An old wives' tale or not, I always leave a whole apple in the storage container alongside my fruit cakes to help keep them moist.

VARIATION To decorate the cake, brush the surface with 1 tablespoon apricot jam and roll out 175 g (6 oz) ready prepared icing. Press firmly on to the cake, trim the edges and decorate with strips of lemon or orange rind. This will add ½ **POINTS** value per slice.

Apple and cinnamon ring

Makes **10** slices **V**

| *POINTS* values per recipe | **25** | calories per slice | **170** |

Preparation time 20 minutes l Baking time 40 minutes

low fat cooking spray

350 g (12 oz) cooking apples, peeled, cored and grated coarsely

2 tablespoons fresh lemon juice

150 g (5½ oz) self raising white flour

1 teaspoon baking powder

½ teaspoon ground cinnamon

50 g (1¾ oz) demerara sugar

50 g (1¾ oz) sultanas

50 ml (2 fl oz) sunflower oil

2 eggs

100 ml (3½ fl oz) skimmed milk

2 tablespoons reduced sugar apricot jam

1 Preheat the oven to Gas Mark 4/180°C/fan oven 160°C. Spray an 850 ml (1½ pint) ring mould with a little low fat cooking spray. Mix the grated apple with the lemon juice.

2 Sift the flour, baking powder and cinnamon into a mixing bowl. Stir in the grated apple mixture, sugar and sultanas. Make a well in the centre of the mixture.

3 Beat together the oil, eggs, milk and jam. Pour this into the well in the dry ingredients and mix everything together.

4 Spoon the mixture into the prepared mould and level the surface with the back of a spoon. Bake for 35–40 minutes, or until the cake is browned, firm and springy to the touch. Cool in the tin for 10 minutes then loosen the edges with a palette knife, and turn it out on to a cooling rack.

TOP TIP Before serving, dust with ½ a teaspoon of icing sugar, if desired. This will not alter the *POINTS* values.

Sticky cranberry gammon

Serves **1**

| **POINTS** values per recipe | **7** | calories per serving | **367** |

Preparation and cooking time 30 minutes

150 g (5½ oz) lean gammon steak, all fat removed
1 teaspoon honey
50 g (1¾ oz) frozen or fresh cranberries
2 teaspoons whole grain mustard
50 g (1¾ oz) mange tout or sugar snap peas
50 g (1¾ oz) green beans
50 g (1¾ oz) peas
salt and freshly ground black pepper

1 Preheat the grill to High and lay the gammon steak on the grill pan. In a small, covered saucepan, heat the honey with the cranberries, 1 teaspoon of the mustard, seasoning and 2 tablespoons of water. Cook for about 3–4 minutes, until the cranberries start to pop.

2 Brush the gammon steak with the cranberry mixture and grill for 5–6 minutes on each side, brushing frequently with the cranberry mixture.

3 Meanwhile, blanch the vegetables for 30 seconds in salted, boiling water and then toss with the remaining teaspoon of mustard and seasoning.

4 Serve the gammon with the vegetables and any remaining sauce poured over.

Italian trifle

Serves **4 V**

| **POINTS** values per recipe | **28** | calories per serving | **270** |

This velvety smooth Italian dessert is absolutely delicious. *Preparation time 5 minutes Chilling time: 30 minutes*

4 trifle sponges
250 g (9 oz) ricotta cheese
100 g (3½ oz) low fat soft cheese
2 tablespoons reduced sugar jam with extra fruit
450 g (1 lb) fresh or frozen mixed strawberries, raspberries and blueberries in total
400 g can of peach slices in juice
2 drops of vanilla essence

1 Line the bottom of a large glass trifle bowl or four individual bowls with the trifle sponges.

2 In a separate bowl, beat together the ricotta, low fat soft cheese and jam.

3 Quarter the strawberries, if using fresh ones, and mix with the other berries, peach slices and juice and vanilla essence in a bowl. Spoon this mixture over the sponges.

4 Spread the cheese mixture evenly over the fruit and decorate with more berries and mint leaves. Refrigerate for at least 30 minutes before serving.

A festive feast

Butterbean and broccoli soup

Serves **4** ❄

| **POINTS** values per recipe | **12** | calories per serving | **160** |

This is a truly satisfying soup – filling, tasty and packed full of nourishment to help keep the winter bugs at bay! Just 100 g (3½ oz) of boiled broccoli contains over half the recommended daily intake of vitamin C. Serve a generous bowlful with a medium slice of fresh crusty brown bread (1 **POINTS** value). Great for the thermos flask too! *Preparation time 15 minutes l Cooking time 20 minutes*

low fat cooking spray
2 rashers, rindless smoked lean back bacon (about 25 g/1 oz each), chopped
1 large onion, chopped
1 garlic clove, crushed
400 g (14 oz) broccoli, chopped roughly
1.2 litres (2 pints) hot chicken or vegetable stock
2 x 420 g cans butterbeans, drained
1 teaspoon dried rosemary (or 1 tablespoon chopped fresh)
salt and freshly ground black pepper

1 Spray a large non stick saucepan with the low fat cooking spray and fry the bacon over a high heat until it is very crispy. Use a slotted spoon to transfer the bacon to a plate lined with absorbent kitchen paper. Set to one side.

2 Turn the heat down, add the onion, garlic and broccoli, cover and cook for 4–5 minutes or until softened, shaking the pan occasionally.

3 Pour in the stock and bring to the boil. Add the beans, rosemary, and season to taste, then cover and simmer for 15 minutes, until the broccoli is tender.

4 Liquidise two-thirds of the soup until smooth. Add the remaining third and liquidise for a short burst to coarsely chop the remaining vegetables. Return to the pan and reheat. Check the seasoning.

5 Ladle the soup into four warmed bowls and scatter on the crispy bacon bits. Serve immediately.

TOP TIP Choose broccoli that has good dark green florets – an indication of freshness and therefore higher nutritional value.

VEGETARIAN OPTION To make this soup suitable for vegetarians, replace the chicken stock with vegetable stock and omit the bacon rashers. You will save 1 **POINTS** value. For a special garnish, sprinkle 1 teaspoon toasted flaked almonds over the soup. This will add ½ **POINTS** value per serving.

Roast Christmas turkey

Serves **6**

| **POINTS** values per recipe | **31** | calories per serving | **325** |

Preparation time 40 minutes l Cooking time 2 hours

2.25 kg (5 lb) turkey
50 g (1¾ oz) streaky bacon rashers
salt and freshly ground black pepper

FOR THE STUFFING
low fat cooking spray
4 shallots, chopped finely
225 g (8 oz) mushrooms, chopped finely
125 g (4½ oz) fresh wholemeal breadcrumbs
2 teaspoons dried tarragon
2 tablespoons reduced sugar marmalade
3 tablespoons fresh orange juice

FOR THE GRAVY
300 ml (10 fl oz) chicken stock
2 tablespoons cornflour
2 tablespoons port

1 Rinse the turkey well and pat it dry thoroughly with kitchen paper. Place it in a large roasting tin.

2 Preheat the oven to Gas Mark 5/190°C/fan oven 170°C.

3 To make the stuffing, spray a medium saucepan with low fat cooking spray and add the shallots. Cook them gently until softened and then add the mushrooms. Cover and cook gently for 5 minutes until the mushrooms are tender. Remove the pan from the heat and mix in the breadcrumbs, tarragon, marmalade and orange juice. Fill the neck cavity of the turkey with the stuffing and then pull the neck flap of skin over the stuffing and tuck it under the bird, securing it with a cocktail stick. Season it well with salt and freshly ground black pepper, and lay the bacon rashers over the breast in a criss-cross pattern.

4 Roast the turkey for 2 hours. When cooked, carefully lift it out of the roasting tin on to a large serving platter. Allow it to rest for 10 minutes before carving.

5 For the gravy, pour the turkey juices into a pan – skim off the fat first. Stir in the stock and bring it to the boil. Mix the cornflour with the port and stir this in. Cook, stirring, until the gravy thickens.

6 Thinly carve the turkey and serve 150 g (5½ oz) of meat per person with 50 g (1¾ oz) of the stuffing, your chosen zero **POINTS** value vegetables and the gravy.

Perfect roast potatoes

Serves **4 V**

| **POINTS** values per recipe | **18½** | calories per serving | **290** |

Always popular, but these have fewer **POINTS** values than the traditional roast potatoes – and taste just as good. *Preparation time 20 minutes l Cooking time 1 hour*

1 kg (2 1b 4 oz) peeled potatoes, each cut into 3 even sized pieces
8 teaspoons olive oil
1 tablespoon plain flour
low fat cooking spray
salt and freshly ground black pepper

1 Boil the potatoes in plenty of boiling salted water for 10 minutes.
2 Preheat the oven to Gas Mark 7/220°C/fan oven 200°C and heat a large baking tray with the olive oil in it.
3 Drain the potatoes and return them to the saucepan. Cover with a lid and shake them about to soften their edges a bit, then sprinkle over the flour, replace the lid and shake again to part-coat.
4 Carefully remove the hot baking tray from oven and transfer the potatoes on to it. Season well and turn the potatoes to coat them in oil. Spray with low fat cooking spray and roast for 30 minutes.
5 Remove from the oven, turn the potatoes, spray again and return to the oven for another 30 minutes after which they should be golden brown and crispy on the outside, but soft in the middle.

Spicy turkey cakes

Serves **4**

| **POINTS** values per recipe | **12** | calories per serving | **150** |

These little cakes are good as an appetiser with drinks. Serve with a fresh tomato, red onion and red pepper salad with lots of lime juice and wedges for no extra **POINTS** values. *Preparation and cooking time 40 minutes*

350 g (12 oz) minced turkey
2 teaspoons red Thai curry paste
1 medium egg, beaten
2 tablespoons cornflour
zest of 2 limes
a small bunch of fresh coriander, chopped
2 spring onions, sliced finely
1 medium red chilli, de-seeded and sliced finely
low fat cooking spray

TO SERVE
lime wedges

1 Put the minced turkey, red curry paste and about half the egg in a food processor and process until evenly blended then transfer to a bowl.
2 Add the cornflour, lime zest, coriander, spring onions and chilli and mix well with your fingers. Add more egg if necessary to bind the mixture.
3 Divide the mixture into 12 portions and roll each into a ball then flatten slightly to make a patty.
4 Heat a large frying pan and spray with the low fat cooking spray. Fry the cakes in batches for about 5 minutes on each side, until golden and cooked through.

VARIATION Try serving these turkey cakes with a salsa, a soy dipping sauce and/or some sweet chilli sauce.

Brussels sprouts with chestnuts

Serves **6 V** *if using vegetarian crème fraîche*

| **POINTS** values per recipe | 5½ | calories per serving | 75 |

Delicious at any time of the year but the perfect seasonal accompaniment to the roast Christmas turkey; see page 165. *Preparation and cooking time 20 minutes*

700 g (1 lb 9 oz) Brussels sprouts, washed and trimmed
100 g pack vacuum sealed chestnuts
4 tablespoons half fat crème fraîche
a pinch of freshly grated nutmeg
salt and freshly ground black pepper

1 Bring a large pan of water to the boil. Make a cross in the bottom of the Brussels sprouts with a sharp knife, add to the water and cook for 10 minutes until just tender.
2 Drain and return to the hot pan. Add the chestnuts, crème fraîche, a pinch of nutmeg and season. Toss together and serve.

Teriyaki turkey noodles

Serves **4** ❄

| **POINTS** values per recipe | 24 | calories per serving | 440 |

Preparation and cooking time 25 minutes + 15 minutes standing

250 g (9 oz) medium egg noodles
600 ml (20 fl oz) boiling chicken stock
3 tablespoons Teriyaki sauce
1 tablespoon vegetable oil
450 g (1 lb) turkey breasts, cut into thin strips
175 g (6 oz) carrots, cut into matchsticks
100 g (3½ oz) celery, sliced thinly
125 g (4½ oz) mange tout peas
1 bunch of spring onions, shredded
2 tablespoons tomato ketchup
2 teaspoons cornflour
2 tablespoons sherry

1 Place the noodles in a bowl. Pour over the boiling stock. Stir in the Teriyaki sauce and leave for 15 minutes.
2 Meanwhile, heat the oil in a large frying pan or wok and add the turkey strips. Stir fry for about 5 minutes and then add the carrots, celery and mange tout peas. Stir fry for a further 5 minutes.
3 Drain the noodles, reserving the liquid, and add them to the pan or wok, with the spring onions, mixing well. Add the reserved liquid and bring to the boil.
4 Mix together the tomato ketchup, cornflour and sherry, and add this to the pan. Cook, stirring, until the sauce thickens a little, and then serve straight away.

Winter vegetable korma

2½ POINTS VALUE

Serves **4 V** ❄ *after step 2*

| **POINTS** values per recipe | **11** | calories per serving | **240** |

Korma is one of the mildest (and creamiest) of curries. Enjoy this 'warm' dish with either 4 tablespoons plain boiled rice (3 **POINTS** values) or ½ medium naan bread for 4 **POINTS** values.

Preparation time 10 minutes l Cooking time 20 minutes

1 tablespoon vegetable oil

2 large onions, sliced

2 garlic cloves, crushed

1 tablespoon ground cumin

1 tablespoon ground coriander

1 teaspoon ground turmeric

1 teaspoon ground ginger or a 4 cm (1½ inch) piece fresh
   ginger, grated

1 tablespoon plain flour

450 ml (16 fl oz) vegetable stock

1 tablespoon tomato purée

225 g (8 oz) carrots, sliced

225 g (8 oz) parsnips, chopped

275 g (9½ oz) cauliflower florets

425 g can chick peas, drained

110 g (4 oz) button mushrooms, halved

4 tablespoons low fat plain yogurt

salt

2 tablespoons chopped fresh coriander or parsley, to garnish

1 Heat the oil in a large pan, add the onions and cook gently for 5 minutes, until softened and golden. Add the garlic and stir in the ground spices. Cook for a minute. Sprinkle on the flour and cook for a further minute.

2 Blend in the vegetable stock until smooth, add the tomato purée, carrots and parsnips. Bring to the boil, cover and simmer for 10 minutes. Add the cauliflower, chick peas and mushrooms and simmer for a further 10 minutes.

3 Season, take the pan off the heat and lightly swirl in the yogurt. Serve garnished with the chopped herbs.

TOP TIP For a hotter curry, add ½–1 teaspoon chilli powder at step 1 with the other spices. For a quick korma, replace all the vegetables with frozen mixed vegetables, adding ½ **POINTS** value per 100 g (3½ oz).

Festive spice cookies

Makes **20** cookies **V**

| **POINTS** values per recipe | **54** | calories per cookie | **175** |

These cookies are especially good for cutting into shapes for Christmas decorations or party treats.
Preparation and cooking time 35 minutes

low fat cooking spray
400 g (14 oz) plain flour
100 g (3½ oz) self raising flour
1 teaspoon baking powder
1 teaspoon bicarbonate of soda
1 teaspoon ground ginger
1 teaspoon ground cinnamon
¼ teaspoon nutmeg
125 g (4½ oz) polyunsaturated margarine
125 g (4½ oz) soft brown sugar
3 tablespoons black treacle
2 tablespoons golden syrup

1 Preheat the oven to Gas Mark 4/180°C/fan oven 160°C and lightly coat a baking tray with the low fat cooking spray.

2 Sift the flours, baking powder, bicarbonate of soda and spices together into a large bowl and make a well in the middle. In a saucepan melt the margarine, sugar, treacle and syrup then pour into the well. Add 2 tablespoons of water and mix together.

3 Turn out on to a floured surface and roll out to about ½ cm (¼ inch) thick. Cut into shapes and place on the baking sheet working quickly while the dough is still warm.

4 Bake for 10 minutes or until the cookies are slightly risen and a dark golden brown. They should still be slightly soft in the middle as they will harden on cooling. If using as decorations, make holes to hang them whilst they are still warm and soft.

5 Transfer to a wire rack to cool then decorate if you wish.

Mincemeat surprises

Makes **15 V** *if using vegetarian mincemeat*

| **POINTS** values per recipe | **30** | calories per tart | **100** |

A lovely winter dish to serve with low fat custard (remember to add the **POINTS** values) and to treat the kids with when they come home from school. *Preparation time 10 minutes l Cooking time 20 minutes*

250 g (9 oz) ready made puff pastry
150 g (5½ oz) luxury mincemeat
caster sugar, to serve

1 Preheat the oven to Gas Mark 6/ 200°C/fan oven 180°C.

2 Roll half the pastry out to fit a small, non stick baking tin.

3 Spread with the mincemeat.

4 Roll out the rest of the pastry and use to top the mincemeat. Sprinkle with a little icing sugar.

5 Bake in the preheated oven for 20 minutes.

6 Cool in the tin for 5 minutes and then cut into 15 portions.

Little Christmas puddings

Makes **8** puddings **V**

| **POINTS** values per recipe | 26½ | calories per serving | 215 |

Serve each little pudding with a spoonful of crème fraîche if you wish; just remember to count the **POINTS** values. *Preparation time 30 minutes + 1 day soaking l Cooking time 1 hour + 1 hour to reheat (or 30 seconds to microwave)*

175 g (6 oz) sultanas

175 g (6 oz) currants

50 g (1¾ oz) glacé cherries, halved

75 ml (3 fl oz) rum or brandy

½ teaspoon polyunsaturated margarine

100 g (3½ oz) carrots, finely grated

75 g (2¾ oz) fresh white breadcrumbs

finely grated zest and juice of 1 small orange

1 teaspoon ground mixed spice

50 g (1¾ oz) unrefined light or dark muscovado sugar

1 egg, beaten

1 Cover the sultanas, currants and cherries with boiling water. Soak for 10 minutes, then drain well. Add the rum or brandy, then cover and soak for 24 hours to swell the fruit.

2 Grease 8 individual pudding basins with the margarine. Add the remaining ingredients to the fruit mixture, and stir well. Spoon into the pudding basins, level the surfaces and cover with circles of greaseproof paper. Secure pieces of foil over each basin.

3 Steam the puddings for 1 hour, topping up the steamer with extra boiling water as required. Never allow the steamer to boil dry and always use boiling water for topping up.

4 Cool the puddings when cooked and replace the pieces of foil with fresh pieces. Store in a cool, dark place. On Christmas Day, steam the puddings for 1 hour to reheat, or microwave on High for 30 seconds per pudding, allowing them to stand for 2 minutes before serving.

Boxing Day muffins

Makes: **12** ❄ **V** *if using vegetarian mincemeat and free-range eggs*

| **POINTS** values per recipe | **32½** | calories per serving | **180** |

A great way to start the day is with these muffins – warm and freshly made – and a mug of home-brewed coffee. They will set you up for a traditional Boxing Day walk! *Preparation time 15 minutes l Cooking time 25 minutes*

110 g (4 oz) fresh cranberries

100 g (3½ oz) mincemeat

1 small apple, peeled, cored and grated

300 g (10½ oz) plain flour

1 teaspoon baking powder

1 teaspoon mixed spice

1 teaspoon ground cinnamon

50 g (1¾ oz) light muscovado sugar

a pinch of salt

1 medium egg, beaten

200 ml (7 fl oz) skimmed milk

3 tablespoons vegetable oil

1 Preheat the oven to Gas Mark 4/ 180°C/fan oven 160°C. Line a muffin tray with twelve paper muffin cases. Place the cranberries, mincemeat and apple in a bowl. Mix together well.

2 Sift the flour, baking powder, spices, sugar and salt in a separate bowl. Put the egg, milk and oil in a jug and whisk together well.

3 Make a well in the centre of the dry ingredients and pour in the egg mixture quickly mixing together until just blended. Do not over mix.

4 Carefully fold in the fruit mixture. Divide between 12 muffin cases. Bake for 20–25 minutes until well risen and golden. Transfer to a wire rack to cool slightly before serving.

TOP TIP If you over mix any muffin mixture, the muffins will become tough, so handle with care!

VARIATIONS Replace the cranberries with 1 medium banana, chopped. Allow 3 **POINTS** values per muffin. Replace the mincemeat with 75 g (2¾ oz) chopped ready to eat apricots. Allow 3 **POINTS** values per muffin.

Index